WHATEVER IT TAKES!

FOR ALL STUDENTS TO SUCCEED IN SCHOOL AND LIFE

By

Dr. Bryan Pearlman

Table of Contents

Introduction

---•◆•---

The majority of my K-12 schooling was nothing short of terrible. My grades were poor, my attendance was poor, and my attitude was even worse. The content and methods utilized were ineffective at meeting my needs. The school day was either way too easy or way too hard. I am certain that I had an undiagnosed learning disability in reading and writing. I do not believe Attention Deficit Hyperactivity Disorder (ADHD) was invented then; if so, I would have been diagnosed with that as well. I was off-task the majority of the school day. At the same time, I was gifted in math. I am sure that my profile made it a challenge to educate me effectively. I also do not believe teachers were lining up to volunteer to have me in their classroom. I definitely don't blame them for that.

I dreaded going to school each day. *Ferris Bueller* had nothing on me. I worked hard to fake just about any possible illness and use just about any excuse possible not to go to school.

In the late 1970s and early 1980s, there was a greater focus on the way a lesson was written, planned, and delivered. There was less focus on how it was received by the students. I remember there being a "special" classroom where those who learned differently were placed. Looking back, there was little commonality between those students. There were students with cognitive delays, visual impairments, behavior challenges, and those with mobility issues. I remember thinking about my friend Scott who was way smarter than I was, but because he utilized a wheelchair, he was placed in that room. Even then, I thought there was something inherently wrong with this model. It was established for convenience, rather than what was in the best interest of the student.

The message I, and I am sure many other, received from witnessing this "special" room was that if you were not in the average to slightly above average range, there was no place for you in a regular classroom. This was the definition of a one-size-fits-all approach, which, unfortunately, did not work too well for me or many other students. This structure and other factors were a significant reason for students to become disenfranchised and to give up on school when they were of age to do so. The dropout rate at that point was nearly double what it is today.

Additionally, research shows that students make their own decision at a very young age about how smart they are, whether or not education is for them, and if they are going to be successful or not. This is a very difficult mindset to change once it is cemented. The percentage of students continuing their education through college was a third lower in the 1970s than today. Tracking students was a common practice and it too was very hard to move from one track to another.

Behavior management, called discipline then, was heavy handed and punitive. There was little focus on the root cause of behaviors. Nobody knew or thought much about traumatic events and how these could influence a student's ability to access the curriculum, succeed at school, or make good choices. I even remember a public school I attended where corporal punishment was permitted (and encouraged). Many students complied to the best of their ability out of fear of being paddled by an adult. At the time, I struggled with understanding why we punished a student for hitting another student by having an adult hit the student with a paddle. Moreover, looking back on this, what if the student was acting out in school because he/she was being beaten up or abused at home by a parent? What if the behaviors were a cry for help because of trauma or a basic human need of attention? What were we teaching and what impact did this have on students?

Mental health related challenges and concerns were not discussed or understood very well in schools. This was left for mental health professionals. Making the situation worse, many families viewed mental health concerns as a stigma and were avoided at all costs. This left many students with moderate or more severe needs to struggle and suffer on their own in silence. I can't possibly imagine how many students were negatively impacted by these practices over the decades.

Students who were distracted or preoccupied were called lazy or daydreamers. There was no sense of urgency to get to know why students were off-task or struggling with school. We blamed the student for something that they had little ability to control. This would be like blaming a student with diabetes for his/her blood sugar being low or someone with asthma for not having enough oxygen in his/her lungs. I remember many of my friends' parents telling their children to toughen up, to get over it, or to stop whining about it. This did not appear to help or to be a good solution for the mental health struggles and challenges that were likely rooted in anxiety or depression. This model fits the "blame the victim" approach.

The structure of school combined with struggling to focus, organization, reading, and writing was a recipe for failure, frustration, and anger for me. I was a frequent visitor to the school principal and the school nurse. My cries for help were not recognized and each day pretty much went according to the same script.

I also struggled with seeing the light at the end of the tunnel. I spent a lot of time thinking about my limitations and learning challenges. A lot of good-natured and well-intended adults thought the best solution was to quadruple dip me in reading and writing interventions. Strangely, this only further reinforced that I could not read or write.

At the same time, it pulled me out of the opportunity for enrichment in math and other electives that potentially could have sparked an interest or unearthed a hidden talent. Those opportunities could have been enough of a success to build off and to help change my perception of my challenges and my opinion of school.

I promised myself then that one day I would become a teacher and then a principal. My goal would be to help kids like me to have hope, be successful, enjoy school, and make something of themselves. It took a lot of work, but I've kept that promise and worked very hard to help struggling students change their life trajectory, and to help them build a love for learning. This has not been an easy task, but it is very worthwhile.

In this book, I will share stories about some of the students that I have encountered over my education career. The students in this book struggled in areas of academics, behaviors, as a result of trauma, mental health concerns, and home environmental impacts.

I hope this book is helpful and I urge you to find students like these in your own school and help change their life trajectory! I encourage you to challenge yourself and your colleagues to always do: *Whatever It Takes! For All Students to Succeed in School and Life!* All kids deserve this commitment.

As Peter Parker was told in Spiderman, "With great power comes great responsibility." Every educator has tremendous power, they can help a student to experience success, have hope for the future, and set them on the right course towards a successful life. I also believe that for students in the worst circumstances, educators can save their life. What could be more important than that?

As you read through this book, you will encounter parts that will make you laugh and cry, but if I'm successful — they will make you feel inspired to take-action, too. You should also leave with several tools and strategies that you can implement immediately.

If questions arise, I encourage you to contact me. I would like nothing more than to help you brainstorm and problem-solve to help a student in need.

Thank you for taking the time to read this book!

Book
Overview/Structure

———————◆———————

So many experts look at students and their behaviors. They develop programs, manuals, and interventions. These are color coded, backed with acronyms, and are quickly gobbled up by the masses — who are all looking for a quick fix to the ails of our school and society. Some of these books fall short, because they are macro-level texts that are aimed to be generalized over many students across the country. They are rich in research and generally lacking in real world application.

My goal in writing this book was to look at specific students and why they struggle. You will see that we discuss what we attempted, what we learned from it, and what research/experts recommend when dealing with this situation and other similar situations. I encourage you to think of students that you are working with or have worked with that are similar to the ones described in this book. You can reflect on what you did, how effective the strategies were, and what you would do differently in the future.

To be clear, this book is not aimed at causing anyone shame, blame, or guilt. I believe that everyone does the best they know how to at a specific point in time. It is critical in the learning cycle to make mistakes, learn from them, and be better equipped for future challenges.

I am only concerned about educators and colleagues that either do not take risks to help students and/or those that repeat the same mistakes by using methods that we know will not produce a positive outcome. As a former teacher once told me, "If we do the same thing over and over again and expect a different outcome with our kids — that's not education that's what we call insanity."

After the case studies, I introduce my approach to ensuring that all students can be successful in school and in life. This is called the **SHOCKERS** approach. I also share eight common things that struggling students have in common along with many suggestions that can help when working with struggling and challenging students.

Whatever It Takes! is a catchy name, a great song title from the band *Imagine Dragons*, and it is my mission in life. Hopefully, after reading this book it will be yours, too!

Case
Studies

Dr. Bryan Pearlman

Bryan

————◆————

ryan was a new student at our school—moving to Boston from Florida. His file was received a few days before the school year started and it was very thick. It became very obvious that Bryan was a complete puzzle to the previous school staff.

A note on the cover of the file read: *"Good luck with this kid!"* Inside the file was a sheet of paper with the following bulleted list:

- calls out frequently (disrupting class)
- easily distracted
- appears bored
- often off-task
- in the nurse's office frequently
- poor penmanship and writing skills
- below grade level in reading
- not meeting potential
- difficulty sitting still
- free/reduced lunch program

- two grade levels ahead in mathematics (highest math assessment in the district)

- qualified for the gifted program?

  (question mark was hand-written in red ink)

- four schools in the past six years

- both parents work long hours — difficult to reach by phone

- loves talking about sports and enjoys PE and recess (favorite sport is tennis)

- regularly refuses to do work and homework is rarely turned in and it is often incomplete

- Sarcastic and sometimes rude

On the first day of school, the principal called Bryan to the office for a beginning of the school year pep talk and introduction. He is impressed by Bryan's manners, his extensive knowledge about sports, and his sense of humor. The principal gives him a school tour and then delivered him back to his class. When finished, the principal took out the file to review it again and decided to call the previous school. He was very puzzled about the disconnect between the file and the student he just met.

The principal checked in multiple times with Bryan during the first week of school and the reports were all positive. Bryan seemed happy during each of these visits.

The second week of school, the principal was heading back to his office from a meeting and spots Bryan sitting on a chair outside his office. There is a note from the teacher saying that Bryan was making "bodily function" noises when they were doing a read aloud. The principal kind of laughed inside a bit remembering when he was a teacher and wondering if he would have sent someone to the office for this. He had a pep talk with Bryan and sent him back to class with instructions to not do that again and to apologize to his teacher.

The next day, Bryan was again sitting in front of the principal's office when he returned from doing a teacher observation. This time he held a note saying that he would not stop calling out answers during math class and he wasn't letting anyone else have a turn. The principal thought again about whether or not this warranted an office referral… well whatever. Either way, he gave Bryan another pep talk and sent him back to class.

Later that day, the principal was heading to the nurse's office—the nurse's office had the only adult bathroom on that floor. As he walked into the office, he noticed Bryan sitting on a chair with a thermometer in his mouth. After using the bathroom, the principal asked the nurse why Bryan was in the office. She stated that Bryan's teacher was concerned because he was complaining of "flu like symptoms."

Over the next few weeks, this "dance" continued. Bryan either got sent to the office for a low-level disruption or he was in the school nurse's office for a health-related concern.

- What would you do for Bryan?
- Why was Bryan in the principal's office and the nurse's office so often?
- What does Bryan need right now?
- If you were his teacher, principal, or nurse what would you have done differently?

Thank you for your help!
That was me 35-plus years ago!

The week before I started my first teaching position, my mom sent me my school file, and all of my report cards. The above story and description is just the shortened, and more positive, version of what I read in those files. When I read the items in my file, I felt horrible and it further cemented my mission and what I knew I had to do as a teacher, and then as an administrator. There were very few positives, few kind words, and a lot of negatives. How did I even stand a chance? I have continued to keep this folder with me as I moved from teacher to assistant principal, to principal, to central office, to my professional development business, and now with me at our non-profit. This is my daily reminder of the importance of the work that we do and why we have to keep up the battle to help struggling students.

JJ

———◆———

I left the classroom after only three years of teaching for my first administrative position. The year before, I was recognized for being a top teacher and an advocate for students. I was involved in all school committees and volunteered for every before- or after-school activity. I truly felt like I could do no wrong. I had a little swagger. In my mind, at the time, I thought that I knew it all. I began applying for administrative positions, since this was the logical next step and it was an important part of keeping the promise to myself. I went on several interviews and I was hired late in the summer for an assistant principal position in a suburban St. Louis elementary school. This was very exciting. I stayed up at night with anticipation, and a bit of nervousness. I assumed it would be much the same as my experience as a fifth-grade teacher. I was naïve and in for a big surprise.

The first day of school was very overwhelming. However, at least I looked the part of an administrator. I had a sports coat and colorful kid-friendly tie on; I had a walkie-talkie on my belt; I carried a clipboard with rosters on it; I had a keyring with thirty-two keys on it; and, I had a newly minted identification badge with my name and impressive title prominently listed on it. The district issued me these tools because they knew I was ready for the challenge (or so I thought).

The majority of our students were dressed in their new clothes. They appeared to be excited to reconnect with their friends, to meet their new teacher, and to get this school year rolling. The last of the buses arrived and I had my introduction and first encounter with JJ. JJ was dressed in dirty clothes, his shoes had holes in them (his big toe was sticking out), he did not have a smile on his face, and he definitely did not look like he was very excited to be at school. JJ got off his bus, turned the other way, and began walking down the sidewalk away from school. This was a new one for me. I decided to chase after him. It took some coercion and convincing from me to get him into school, but it took a bit more time to get him to class. Eventually, I was able to get him settled in to his class and we started the school day with the announcements.

Later, I happened to run into the school counselor and I asked her about JJ. She was not surprised that there was already an issue. The counselor told me that JJ's story began with some major losses in his life. He was very little when two of his siblings died in a fire. JJ survived but had severe asthma as a result of exposure to inhaling a great deal of smoke. Mom fell out of the picture and his grannie raised him the best she knew how. But, in reality, the streets raised JJ.

JJ was a "frequent flyer" to the counselor and office. Some of these visits were due to disrupting the class (his teacher said that he was off-task one-hundred percent of the time), some were due to work refusal, work avoidance, and others were daily stops on his wandering around the building tour. As difficult as JJ's behaviors could be in class, there was something very likeable about him. He was a salesman, negotiator, and finagler. JJ had a presence about him and an aura. He had great eye contact, a big smile, and an infectious laugh. If you asked most of the school staff about JJ, they would admit their frustration with his behaviors but would also tell you how much they liked him. JJ was also a great kickball player and could practically kick the ball a mile.

JJ's teachers and the school staff spent a lot of extra time with him, providing in-class interventions for math, reading, and writing.

The day before winter break, JJ was sent to my office for being extremely disrespectful to a substitute teacher. I laid into him. I lectured him and told him about how disappointed I was. The conversation went on to how many people were in his corner and how, maybe, he was just wasting their time if he wasn't going to step up and do the right thing. Maybe there were more deserving kids for all of the resources that we had set-up for him.

JJ cried for the first time that anyone at school could remember. He promised that he would do better and that he was sorry for letting everyone down. He even said that he really appreciated everything that was being done for him.

I was so proud of myself for sticking it to JJ. I believed that I wouldn't have any more trouble with him. Other teachers heard about me making JJ cry and they too were happy and gave me high five's and a pat on the back. On the ride home, I called my wife Lena and told her about how I put JJ in his place (she had heard so many stories about him in the past). In my mind, I put this day down as a big one in the win column.

Winter break was going so well. I was having a great time with my wife and children. I truly could not think of a time that I was more relaxed or happy in a very long time. Life could not get any better for me or my family. I even reflected on how much the school year had improved as the days went on.

A few days later, on Christmas day, I received a phone call from my head principal. I could hear in her voice that something was wrong. She did not sound like herself and it seemed as though she was crying and struggling to get words out. She then told me that JJ experienced a severe asthma attack earlier in the day and died in the ambulance on the way to the hospital. I froze and did not say a word. I don't remember hanging up the phone or leaving the room. I thought I had heard this wrong. I had never lost a student in my short career. My emotions ran the full spectrum. This news hit me like a ton of bricks. At that moment, all I could think about was the last conversation that

I had with him. The last thing that was conveyed to JJ was that he was a bad kid, he was wasting our time, he had very little value, and that his behaviors needed to change in order to be accepted at this school. My emotions moved from disbelief, to sadness, to disappointment, to anger, to a huge hole, and then at some point I accepted this and thought about what I had to do for the staff, for JJ's family, and for his friends and fellow fifth-graders.

Driving the thirty-minute ride to the funeral home felt like an eternity. As difficult as JJ was, school would not be the same without him. In fact, a good part of the staff's day and school week had been spent dealing with JJ. Our school would be down only one student out of 500 on the roster; however, this loss was going to be noticed, felt, and hard to deal with in the future.

At the funeral home, there were large photos of JJ prominently displayed. There he was with the big smile, the braided hair, and the light eyes with a little mischief in them. It was a surreal moment. It was hard to believe that he was gone. I found a seat in the back and tried to stay unnoticed. I kept my sunglasses on because I could feel the tears swelling up. I rarely cried at all in my life and can't remember a time that I cried in public. I was hoping to hold it together, offer my condolences, and re-group at home to figure out what needed to be done to help everyone in the school community to deal with this news.

JJ's grandmother stood up and said how much JJ loved going to that elementary school. How she understood that he had been a challenge for the staff, but that everyone went well above and beyond to help him be successful. She said how much JJ loved recess and especially playing kickball with his friends. She went on to say that his favorite person was Dr. Bryan Pearlman, the assistant principal. His grandmother looked right at me and smiled. She said thank you for caring about JJ and for holding him accountable. His grandmother stated that on many occasions JJ told her about how much Dr. Pearlman liked and cared about him.

I felt like a complete fraud. Beneath my sunglasses, I began to cry. I was the administrator that a week ago tore him down, made him cry, and, worse yet, I was proud of myself for doing it.

JJ died over ten years ago. If he was still alive, he would be finishing up with college.

I think about JJ every day. For a long time, I was mad at myself for leaving things the way I did and for making him cry. I wondered if I could have one more day with JJ, what else I could have done to help him succeed academically and behaviorally. How I wish I could have told him about his amazing strengths and the great future he could have with his amazing smile, his innate ability to negotiate, and his communication skills. He truly could have been successful at just about anything he set his mind toward. I now think about the impact of trauma on JJ and how that impacted his behaviors. I realize now how poorly equipped I was to handle this. Most of my strategies, tools, and methods involved "carrots and sticks." Nothing that I did addressed his mental health needs and concerns, or the many Adverse Childhood Experiences (ACEs) that he experienced. I also never considered alternatives to suspensions. Shame on me. I should have known all of these tools were ineffective and that we were simply repeating the same mistakes over and over again and expecting a different outcome. Insanity!

I committed to sharing his story with as many people as I could. I also committed to helping educators to better understand trauma and how to help students with trauma and challenging behaviors to be successful in school and life. We can't waste a day, an hour, or even a minute! And I truly believe that we have to do *Whatever It Takes* (for each and every student every day)—there is no guarantee for tomorrow. No excuses and no regrets!

- What would you have done if you had been in my shoes?
- What tools and strategies could we have used to help him be more successful?
- What role could trauma-responsive methods have played in working with JJ?
- What role could training in mental health, behavior challenges, and best practices have played in helping these situations?

Later in the book, we will help answer these and other trauma-related questions.

Annie

———◆———

I remember only a few things from my undergraduate child psychology class. One of the things I do remember is that children require love and attention. I also remember hearing that any attention was better than no attention. This is a biological and basic human need, just like the need for oxygen, water, food, and shelter. So, it would be logical that if a student receives no attention from loved ones and other adults, that they will do whatever they can to get attention. This helps them know that they exist.

Annie was a new student to our school at the beginning of the school year. She was a first-grader in Mrs. Ray's classroom (room nine). Annie's records had not yet been received by our school. She was assigned to a class very randomly since we knew very little about her.

The school year started and on the first day we had planned a welcome back and welcome new family members' assembly. This was a time when we made everyone feel like a part of the school family. For most students, this was a high-energy, highly engaging, and fun time. This definitely fit in as a preferred activity.

In a school of almost 600 elementary students, it is sometimes hard to stand-out. Quite honestly, sometimes students fly under the radar. Not Annie… It did not take long for staff and administration to become aware of her. In the middle of the first school assembly, she got up ran around the gym and exited the building through the hallway door. This was only our very first of many encounters with Annie.

As the first few weeks went by, we came to understand that Annie does what she wants to do when she wants to do it. The school rules, norms, and procedures do not appear to apply to her. Many of Annie's behaviors made school staff question whether or not this first-grader had ever attended a school. Her behavior more closely resembled that of a preschool student. Annie was a frequent flyer to the office. She couldn't sit still in her classroom and she annoyed other students (and, honestly, annoyed all of her teachers, too). Within the first month of school, Annie had been sent to the office ten times and had three out-of-school suspended days.

When Annie came back to school, she was more upset and further behind. The school had become a revolving door with Annie. She came to school, made bad choices and violated a school policy, then she got suspended, came back to school in worse shape than she left, and repeated again and again.

Looking back, this whole approach seems silly. Actually, as mentioned in the previous chapter, it too is the definition of insanity, since many of us thought that even though we were repeating the same steps, in some way there had to be a different outcome. Many excused this insanity by stating that we had no other choices and that we certainly could not allow these behaviors to continue. One staff member asked if there was a possibility to move this six-year-old back to preschool or to the district's alternative school. I have been told that in the brainstorming process, there are no bad ideas. Forget that, these were not just bad ideas—they were awful ideas. Preschool would have been devastating to whatever small bit of dignity or self-worth that Annie had left. The alternative school featured high school students, many of whom had major fights, significant disruptive behaviors, and in some cases alcohol possession charges in their file. Not a good fit for Annie, even though she had as many suspended days as these students had in their file.

A bit more about Annie. She was enduring some major life challenges. She had been passed back and forth to different caregivers. Best case scenario was that she believed her mom is very busy, but a more likely scenario was that she knew her mom didn't care about her at all and did everything possible to have nothing to do with her. It was not uncommon for her to go weeks without seeing or hearing from her mother.

Adding to this situation was the fact that the other caregivers didn't care very much for her either. They fed her and put a roof over her head, but they too wanted very little to do with her. It really was a situation where someone gets "stuck" with her until she could get pawned off on another relative.

Annie's home existence was one of very little contact with others, and no love or support. The little contact she did get was negative reinforcement—which included a great deal of yelling, frustration, and punishments. She struggled with academics. She struggled with behaviors. Annie was dying for even the smallest amount of attention, love, and kindness. The few times that Annie saw her mom was always as a result of a very poor choice that Annie made. Whomever the caregiver was at the time would get ahold of mom and insist that she come immediately to deal with this "devil child." Within hours, mom arrived, located Annie, beat her until she cried and then mom finally gave up due to exhaustion. Then Mom leaves and Annie goes to her room crying. This same process was repeated frequently.

Even with all that, somehow Annie still got out of bed, would take the hour bus ride to school, and walk into our building every day. It should also be noted that Annie showed interest in the people who worked in the cafeteria and she also had a relative strength in basic mathematics.

We were at the point when we were most frustrated, out of tools, throwing our hands-up, and ready to give up on Annie. The next day I noticed that it was a bit quieter than usual. My morning visit with Annie had not occurred. Why hadn't a teacher brought her to my office? Why can't I remember giving her the pep talk as she hoped off the bus? What was going on? I got up and was heading through the office when my secretary gave me a note with a call back message. It was Annie's caregiver. I was puzzled. The only times I ever received a call from her caregivers was in response to me leaving them a message to come get Annie on route to a multiple day suspension.

I immediately called Annie's caregiver. She told me they had decided to leave to visit family in Memphis. I asked about how long Annie would be gone. The caregiver said that it could be up to a week or so. Annie's teachers were a bit relieved, since their week would most likely be more tolerable and it would be likely that the other students would actually be able to learn while not being interrupted by Annie's antics. I personally feel bad to say this, but I was relieved a bit, too. I knew that I would have more time out of my office and could visit more classrooms. This was because most days when Annie was in school, she spent several hours a day in my office. I sometimes thought that I was one of the highest paid and overqualified "babysitters" in the county.

A few days later, my secretary came to my office. She looked a little more confused and puzzled. She told me that she just received a records request from a school in Tennessee. I thought for a second and couldn't figure out why that was out of the ordinary. We had at least seventy-five students move in and out of our building during each school year. This was a weekly occurrence. The reason for the puzzled look was that this record request was for Annie.

At once, I tried to call Annie's caregiver but the line was disconnected. I then called the school listed on the record request. They confirmed Annie had toured the school and that the plan was for her to start there the next day, as soon as they were in receipt of the records request.

Looking back, I am surprised that my first reaction was not one of relief. I remember feeling really bad that Annie was not going to be coming back. The thoughts that came to mind included the imaginary stories that she shared with me, the thousands of questions she asked me when she was supposed to be quietly contemplating the bad choices she'd made, the many times she tried to finagle and negotiate with me, and the times she literally fell asleep mid-sentence hanging halfway off the chair. As challenging as her behaviors were, I really missed her and still do. She was just a little kid who had been dealt a bad hand. To this day, I think about Annie and in a very hopeful way consider that with her strong survival skills and personality that she really had a decent chance at making it. I truly hope that I am right.

- What would you have done if you had been in our shoes?
- What tools and strategies could we have used to help Annie be more successful?
- What opportunities did we miss?

– Were there any relative strengths that we could have capitalized on?

– What role could training in mental health, behavior challenges, and best practices have played in helping these situations?

Buck

My family moved about every eighteen months to two years since my dad was in the retailing field. I was told that retailing families were a lot like military families (lot of moves and lots of new schools). I attended eight different schools during my K-12 education. I knew how hard it was to adjust, make new friends, and become acclimated to a new school and community.

As a principal, I made it a point to greet every new student that started at our school during the year. I gave them a tour and my business card. I really can't remember when I started giving the business card, but in some way, it made the student feel special. I wanted to be sure that each new student knew they had at least one connection or contact at the new school.

In mid-November, we had a new student start at our school. The new student's name was Buck, and he was in the second grade. Buck and his family relocated to the area from Colorado. I really enjoyed giving Buck a tour of the school. He had great manners, was very enthusiastic, and seemed very bright. The parents did not say much but seemed happy to be in our school and the new community. Buck liked our treehouse library, the snakes from the St. Louis Zoo that were in the recently converted fish tank, and our shiny new playground equipment.

During Buck's first week of school, he was a model student. He demonstrated positive character traits, participated in all learning activities, and quickly made many friends. Data from the initial progress monitoring tools and subject pre-assessments, showed that Buck performed at the high-average level. To the school staff, there was nothing remarkable about Buck; he truly blended in well with other students.

I remember running into Buck a few times that first week and each time he greeted me courteously with a big smile. He told me how much he liked our school compared to his last school. When I inquired deeper, he said that everyone at his last school was mean and that he got in trouble a lot. I certainly was confused. Honestly, this left me thinking about what was wrong with the last school. Something didn't add up. Well, whatever the case. It was just very nice to have this young man in our school.

During Buck's second week of school things began to change. Buck's class was heading from gym class back to the classroom and a student cut in front of him in line and Buck punched him in the nose so hard that it made a loud cracking noise. The other student's nose would not stop bleeding for almost an hour. He looked like a boxer who had just

Dr. Bryan Pearlman

stepped out of the ring. The only thing missing was a corner man with cotton balls and an ice pack.

Buck was brought to my office. He started crying and put his head in his lap. After crying non-stop for thirty minutes, Buck looked up at me and said he was sorry. I asked him several questions and he had a hard time answering any of them. He looked genuinely remorseful and had absolutely no idea why he reacted so aggressively to the other student cutting in front of him in the line. He then asked if he could go back to his classroom to get his backpack and jacket. When asked why, Buck said he will need these things because he knew that I would be calling his mom and suspending him—just like the other school did all the time.

I did call his mom to come pick him up that day. Since it was a Thursday afternoon, I let her know that Buck would be out on Friday and that he could return to school on Monday. I asked that she bring him on Monday and meet with me first thing, so that we could set him up for success.

On Monday, Buck and his mother came to my office. He had some letters that he had written while he was out of school. One was an apology letter to the other student and the other letter was to me. The apology letter was written perfectly, with feeling, and with a very colorful drawing on it. I don't think any of us could have asked for more. The letter to me had a plan for how he would handle any similar

32

challenging situations the next time. I thanked him for owning up to what he had done and for his attempts to make the situation right. I went with Buck to his class and he apologized. His apology was well stated, he made perfect eye contact, and he had no excuses. He completely owned his actions and took full responsibility. The other student accepted his apology with a handshake. He told Buck that it was kind of funny because his dad told him he looked like a raccoon with the black eyes. The two turned around and walked to their desks. I left them in the capable hands of their teacher and started the school day.

About an hour later, the teacher did not call on Buck when his hand was raised during math. Buck responded by calling the teacher some bad words, turning over his desk, and throwing a book at the teacher. I was called to the classroom to pick Buck up. When we got back to my office, Buck sat down, put his head in his lap and cried again for about twenty minutes. I asked the school secretary to call down to the room to collect Buck's belongings. I called his mom and she came and got Buck. As we walked out of the office, I told them that he could come back on Wednesday, but that I would like to meet with them when he returned.

On Wednesday, Buck and his mom came in to my office. He had prepared two new cards—one for his teacher and one for me. Buck read these to me and again seemed to feel bad about what happened, and he also articulated a plan for how today would be different. Off to class he went. Mom waited and then she too apologized to me. She threw her hands up and said that she really didn't know what to do. She said that he really was a good kid most of the time.

The morning was kind of quiet. I went by the class to check on Buck a few times. Each time he was working hard in his class. His teacher said that it had been a good morning so far. I was supervising recess and I checked in on Buck again. He was playing basketball with a few of his new friends. Buck said that this was going to be his best year ever and that he loved our school. Recess ended, the students lined up, they went to wash their hands, and they went to the cafeteria for lunch. I went back to my office to meet with a teacher. About two minutes later, I received a "911" distress call from the recess monitor. I moved very quickly to the cafeteria and I saw Buck running on our field away from the school. I caught up to him and convinced him to come to my office. He complied, sat down in the seat and cried for forty minutes. As he was sitting and crying in my office, I had the assistant principal find out what had happened. The report I received was that the cafeteria ran out of ranch dressing. This upset Buck. He quickly lost control. He knocked over several trays and threw a chair at the wall so hard it broke into pieces. He then screamed out a number of bad words and ran out of the building.

We followed the same process as the last two occurrences: Mom picked him up and I informed her that because of the damage to school property and the safety violation of leaving the school, that Buck would be out for a week. Mom did not argue, Buck apologized, and they left.

Over the next few weeks, we had several other occurrences. During one of his weeklong suspensions, we gathered a team to meet to discuss Buck. As a group, we struggled with what plans or interventions could be implemented since there was no consistent or clear cause of the behaviors. Each time the antecedent was different. The time of day, subject in class, and another person involved varied. The only commonality was that something random upset Buck and he overreacted in a very disproportionate way. These overacting behaviors involved harm or damage to a student or to property. We realized that the plans and consequences were ineffective at reducing the explosive behaviors. We also realized that the strategies and interventions were unnecessary when Buck was calm and working productively. Buck was the definition of a student with polar opposite behaviors. He was either a model dream student or a violent and disruptive student. There was no in between behaviors.

- What would you have done if you had been in my shoes?

- What tools and strategies could we have used to help Buck to be more successful?

- What role could training in mental health, behavior challenges, and best practices have played in helping these situations?

Mikey

———◆———

I started a new principal position in a district a lot closer to my home. It was an amazing situation and I was so excited to start the school year. I was working hard to get to know the different students in the building, but one name kept coming up as someone that I needed to meet. His name was Mikey.

Mikey was a third-grade student in our large suburban school district. He was bright and very talented in music. In fact, the music teacher stated that she believed that Mikey had more talent in one hand than any student she has ever taught had in their whole body.

The first few days of school were very busy. There were so many little things that needed to get done, many reports required by central office, and just the normal school operations. I had sort of forgotten to meet Mikey. At the time, I was not too concerned, as I had seen a few other students for behaviors, but not Mikey. I hadn't even looked up his file yet. We made it through the first week of school. I reflected over the weekend and was pretty proud of our staff and how things went. I even remember calling a colleague and discussing how great this year was going to be and surprisingly how easy things had been so far.

The second week of school was a different story. It started off with a bang. Mikey caused a big disruption in his class, stole items from his teacher, punched another student, and tore down and broke a framed piece of artwork from the hallway wall. This all occurred within a five-minute time period as Mikey was heading to the office. As Mikey arrived in the office, I had the opportunity to introduce myself. Before I could even get the words out, he said that he did not do anything and that this was all a big misunderstanding. We went to my office and had a conversation together. Mikey admitted nothing except that he had gotten in trouble with the last principal a lot. It was Mikey's belief that the previous principal was out to get him. Mikey's mom was called and a few hours later right before dismissal, she picked Mikey up. He was suspended for two days for disrupting the class, physically assaulting another student, stealing items, and destroying school property.

During Mikey's suspension, I took the time to review his school history documents. His documents almost filled an entire drawer in a filing cabinet. He had a large binder for each year of school. The common thread between these documents was that he was disruptive, disconnected, depressed, and determined to do only what he wanted to do during the day. One note really stood out, "Mikey is a completely disruptive student. He is off-task almost 100 percent of the time. Mikey is lacking social skills, he does not play well with others, and he does not follow any of the school rules."

Over the school year, his behaviors became more extreme, and in response, so did the consequences. Nothing seemed effective at minimizing the disruptions and helping to keep things safe in the school with Mikey. The school year ended and for two-weeks there was peace and quiet in the building.

On the first day of summer school, Mikey's mom arrived with Mikey. He had not enrolled in summer school, which honestly made the staff very happy, since his behaviors were scary and dangerous. The district policy was that students could be added up to the first day of summer school if there was space remaining. There were two spots open and Mikey got one of them. It definitely did not take long for his behaviors to return.

During the second day of summer school, Mikey attempted to strangle another student with his "casted arm" in the bathroom. This was only stopped because another student walked in and ran to get help. Mikey was brought to the office, his mother was contacted, and he was set to be suspended from summer school for a week. While waiting in the office, he started digging through the secretary's desk. The school secretary stopped him and informed me about this behavior. Mikey's mother picked him up from school.

After school, the school secretary could not find her wallet. She realized at that point that Mikey was the only person in the office and near her desk. The principal and the school resource officer went to Mikey's home. They were greeted at the door by Mikey's mom. She said that Mikey had left to walk to the grocery store to pick-up some things that they needed. They told her that they would go to the store to speak with him. When they arrived at the grocery store, Mikey was finishing checking out and had a bag full of items. The officer noticed that Mikey was using what looked to be the school secretary's credit card. They took him aside and he admitted to stealing the wallet and using the credit card. He also stated that he threw the wallet into the lake behind his house. Mikey said that he did this because the school secretary ratted him out and her actions made the situation worse for him. Mikey was taken to a juvenile hall and had a court date set.

While this was going on, I officially suspended him for the remainder of summer school, for ten days of school to start the school year and requested that the superintendent add on the maximum days allowed by district/state policy. After the court date, the district superintendent held a behavior hearing. Mikey was suspended for an additional month of school. Admittedly, I was a bit disappointed that it was not longer, but at least it would give the staff time to get the school year started and some time to come up with a plan for Mikey's success.

In the interim, we were hosting a character education conference. I had the honor of having lunch with one of the national experts on character education. He asked me about the school and about the kids. Somehow, we got on the subject of challenging kids. Mikey's name came up. I had stated that nothing we tried was working. I also shared that by the time Mikey returned, he was going to have taken over first-place as the all-time leader in most suspended days by an elementary school student in our district of almost thirty thousand students and a district that had been in existence for over fifty years. This was not a distinction that would have made anyone proud and there was no trophy for this. Additionally, due to a handful of students, including Mikey, my school was now in the lead for most suspensions. This too did not make me proud. I had colleagues send me sarcastic emails and leave me voicemails. Apparently, a memo went out stating that as a district we had too many suspended days. I, along with my school, was prominently featured on this memo of shame.

The national character expert listened to lots of information about Mikey. He heard about what didn't work and about everyone's frustration. His response was that we should consider trying to do something to connect him. His belief was that behaviors like this had a lot to do with being an outcast in our school "society." He went on to say that perhaps we should give him a job that required way more trust and authority than he deserved. I must not have reacted well to this suggestion because the expert said that I didn't appear to like his idea. He responded by asking about what we had to lose by trying it. While discussing the plan, the character expert asked if perhaps

Mikey could help with arrival and dismissal duty. I right away thought about what a horrible idea this was. By all means, let's give this foul-mouthed boy a walkie-talkie twice a day and a large audience. I told the expert that this student used words that even made me blush (and I had been a hockey player and heard some real doozies in my day).

I really worried about this plan and also wondered how this national expert became an expert. I even asked him if he really went to school for this. He smiled and encouraged me to try it. As I sat there during the afternoon, I remember deciding that we should give the plan a shot. It certainly couldn't hurt anything, make the situation much worse, and we might as well try since nothing else worked. Why not try out of the box, since in the box strategies were completely unsuccessful?

Mikey returned to school after his suspension on a Friday. The staff worked hard to get him re-acclimated to school and to get him through the day. It was actually a fairly uneventful day. Right before the end of the day, I called Mikey to the office. Before I could say anything, he looked mad and said that he hadn't done anything bad today. I then told him about the help I needed with arrival and dismissal duty. I let him know that this had been one of my weaknesses and that we really needed help to make things run better. I officially offered him the job—though it paid no salary, there were no fringe benefits, and definitely no paid vacation (he already had many official and unofficial vacations this year). Mikey thought about it and agreed to do it.

Before he left for the day, I gave him an old neon orange safety monitor vest that I found in the school basement in an old beat-up box from the 1980s. I gave him the only badge I could find—it said something like "lil" captain. (I'm pretty sure it was a giveaway from a safety fair.) Whatever the case, it was a badge and it did look somewhat official. I also gave Mikey a walkie-talkie. These were the only "tools" I could find for his new job. He said thank you and put his new items into his backpack. In a strange way, he actually looked excited about this new career opportunity.

I went home for the weekend and felt as though the day went way better than I thought it would. By Monday morning, I had actually forgotten about the plan and my new worker—Mikey. I was getting set-up in my office for the day when I heard a vehicle pull up and in looking out the window, I recognized that it was Mikey in his mom's mini-van. I'd seen his mom on many occasions picking him up (because he was in trouble), but she had never dropped him off unless he was serving a bus suspension. I thought this was a bit weird. The mini-van door opened and out walked Mikey with a dry cleaner bag on a hanger held over his shoulder. He came straight to my office.

At that point, I remembered the plan and was thinking I needed to let Mikey know he didn't have to show up an hour before school started to do his job. A big part was because I certainly did not want to have to supervise him for an additional hour. Most days, I already felt like his teacher of record due to the hundreds of hours of "quality time" we spent together when he was sent to my office.

Once in my office, Mikey set the bag down, pulled out a perfectly ironed orange vest and a very shiny "lil" captain badge. He also showed me that his mom had created a name label for him to put on his walkie talkie. Mikey put on his uniform and got himself together, created a check off sheet for buses, and then went out to his post. At first I was in a bit of shock that he was taking this job so seriously and that he actually seemed excited to take on this new role in school. Along with my excitement, I was still a bit skeptical. I took a deep breath and hoped that this wasn't going to be a huge mistake. My mind filled with what could go wrong and also the kind of emails and voicemails I would receive from my colleagues if Mikey made a really bad choice in front of students, parents, and others. I cleared my head of negativity and thought, "What is the worst thing that could happen?"

The school arrival and dismissal process never ran smoother. Mikey was really "on the job." He looked proud in his ironed orange vest and his shiny badge. After a while, other students started to share positives about Mikey. He had others sit with him at lunch and play with him at recess. Previously, he was avoided like the plague as students were afraid that he would hurt them. I had many parents provide positive feedback about the nice young man who was polite and doing such a great job at arrival and dismissal. The superintendent visited our school and went out of his way to add in his weekly memo that he loved the new student led arrival and dismissal program at our school. I received a ton of emails and voicemails. Instead of the predicted ridicule, it was requests to learn more about the program and the young man who led this program. A parent who worked for the local newspaper even did a story about our new student leadership program. The newspaper had a nice colorful photo of an elementary student in a bright orange vest with a shiny badge and embossed walkie talkie. Mikey's negative behaviors almost completely disappeared. He managed to make it through the remainder of the year without a single suspended day. I called the national character expert and thanked him for his wisdom and apologized for my initial skepticism and sarcasm. Who knew?

- What would you have done if you had been in my shoes?
- Why did this plan work?
- What other opportunities could there be for students with similar behaviors to Mikey?
- What role could training in mental health, behavior challenges, and best practices have played in helping these situations?

Dawn

———◆———

I was really enjoying my third day as a brand-new school administrator. The craziness of the start of the school year was over. Things had settled down and surprisingly the transition from teacher to administrator was going pretty smoothly. I was reviewing some school data while sipping on a very large and highly-caffeinated diet soda. Moments later there was a knock at my door and our school secretary informed me that the FBI was in the main office and would like to speak to me.

My first reaction was that I was being "punked" or "hazed." I decided to play along. I really wasn't sure what to expect. I was wondering which of my friends or colleagues were in the office checking in to see how their pal the principal was doing. So, I walked into the main office, there were indeed two FBI agents. They looked just like agents do on television and in movies. The agents introduced themselves and asked if I could speak with them in a quiet place.

I led them to my office and closed the door. The FBI agents told me they were concerned about one of our students and that they would like to speak with her. They stated that she was a five-year old and

45

her name was Dawn. I asked them if they could let me know what the situation was. They stated that it was a matter that had to do with Dawn's family. The agents said they would rather not say anything else at this point. I let them know that it was protocol for me to sit in with this student. The agents looked at each other and nodded. One of the officers said that this was not a problem.

I felt badly that I had not met Dawn yet. I looked her up in our student information system and learned that she was in Ms. Smith's Kindergarten class — room twelve. I let the officers know that I would go to the classroom and bring her to the office.

The two officers asked Dawn a number of benign questions to begin with that Dawn answered. They then asked some questions about her mom, her mom's boyfriend, her grandparents, and her uncle. Dawn had nothing remarkable to say about any of them. It seemed as though these were answers that we would expect from any five-year old. The officers thanked her and let me know that they were done. I asked the officers to hang tight for a moment as I returned Dawn to her classroom.

When I returned to the office, I pressed the officers to give me some more information so that I could know what my next steps would be if there was a problem or issue. The agents stated that Dawn, her mom, and her mom's boyfriend recently moved to town. Dawn's family was living with her grandfather and uncle. The agents said that their colleagues just raided the home an hour before. The grandfather and uncle had been under investigation for months. They were two of the largest distributors of child pornography in the country. The agents were wanting to ensure that Dawn was not involved in this.

Fortunately, Dawn had not been involved or impacted by the activities of her grandfather and uncle. However, the family confiscated the home and Dawn's immediate family was now homeless. With some coordination, the school district and community organizations helped support the family in finding a new place to live. Dawn struggled a bit with the situation because she didn't understand why her grandfather and uncle were gone. She stated many times that she missed them. I am sure one day when she is older the situation will make a lot more sense to her.

- How can we prepare staff and administrators for issues from outside school that impact our students?
- What would you have done if you had been in my shoes?
- What tools and strategies could we have used to help her be more successful?
- What role could training in mental health, behavior challenges, and best practices have played in helping these situations?

Austin "350"

————— ◆ —————

My first encounter with Austin occurred after our Popsicles with the Principal event a week or so before the school year started. I was a new principal in the building and district that year. Austin's mom had apparently dropped him off for the family event an hour early and then left to run a "quick errand." This event was extremely well attended. There had to have been at least 400 people on our playground and field. The majority of the students and families came and left by 6:45 pm.

The event was scheduled to officially end at 7 pm. By 9 pm, there was still no sign of Austin's mom. We brought Austin into the office. We tried calling, texting, and emailing his mom, his other emergency contacts, and even tried to reach a neighbor. We were unsuccessful at reaching anyone.

Austin seemed unaffected either way and had nothing much to say to me. We called the police to see if they could assist us in locating his mom. By 9:45 pm, mom arrived in her car followed by the police officer. She said that she had run some errands and had lost track of time. Mom smelled like cigarette smoke and I asked the officer if he could smell alcohol or marijuana. The officer said that it was too hard to tell, but that he wouldn't put it past her. Apparently, he had already had the pleasure of interacting with Austin's mom on multiple occasions involving noise disturbances, possession of narcotics, public intoxication, shoplifting, and other offenses. The officer stated that the department had a lot of history with this parent.

Mom walked over to Austin and attempted to give him a hug. Austin said, "I guess you forgot about 350." I had no idea what this meant but his mom looked upset. She yelled at him to get in the car. She came over to me and introduced herself and then apologized. Mom stated that this had never happened before and that she really just lost track of time and felt bad that this was our first interaction. They left and I thanked the officer. I packed up and left too, since the next morning was our first day of back to school teacher training and I had a forty-five-minute ride home still in front of me.

The next day I asked around about Austin in between training sessions. Most teachers responded that he was a challenging student who didn't seem to care about anything. They had less than positive things to say about his mother. I also learned that he was a fifth-grade student. This surprised me because he was so much smaller than the other students. The other information I learned about Austin was that he always wore a "hoodie" with the hood pulled tight on his head. He did not get along with any of the other students. Austin usually refused to do his work. He was not generally disruptive, but he just did not do anything during the day. Austin moved slowly through the school and appeared to be lethargic. Occasionally, he would break a school rule, would be disrespectful, or would attempt to walk out of the building.

I kept thinking about Austin during the several days of teacher training. I put a note in my calendar that I would check-in on Austin and see if I could do anything to help him.

The school year started with a great amount of enthusiasm. The first day went amazingly well. I was actually surprised how quiet it was. About thirty minutes before the end of the school day, the PE teacher called the office and asked that an administrator come to the gym to help her. Austin was in the gym sitting in the fetal position with his hood pulled completely over his head. He was non-responsive and would not budge.

I finally convinced him to come with me to the office with the promise that I would not bother him. I just wanted him to be safe. He sat in the office in that same state for about ten minutes.

Finally, Austin stood up and sat in a chair across from me. He asked me if he could just stay at school and not go home. I was puzzled and asked Austin some questions. He said that his home life sucked and that nobody loved or even liked him. He also said he was tired of his mom yelling at him for no reason. Austin said the worst thing is that his mom calls him "350." I tried to get him to explain what this meant, and he clammed up. I figured I would not push my luck. I was very happy to get him talking at all. I planned to inquire again about this once I had the chance to build some more trust and rapport with him.

I wanted to keep him talking so we talked about things that he liked. After some prodding, he said that he really liked superheroes and turtles. I shared with him that I had collected turtles since I was a young child. I showed him the dozen or so turtles in my office. He thought they were really cool. Austin told me that he liked turtles because he used to have a turtle as a pet when he was younger until the turtle died and his mom would not replace it. He asked me why I liked turtles. I told him that someone told me as a kid that they were good luck and I began collecting them and never really stopped acquiring them. I gave him one to take with him. He asked if I thought it might bring him good luck and I told him that I bet it would. Before he left for the day, I asked if he would like to check-in with me each day to just see how we were doing and to see if the turtle brought him any good luck. Austin smiled and said that he would really like that. I sent an email out letting his teachers know that we would be meeting for a few minutes each day for a check-in.

Over time, Austin began to open up. He shared bits and pieces of things from his days. After a while, he stopped wearing the hoodie over his head. At lunch and recess, I noticed that he even started to engage a little with other students. I checked with teachers and they said that he was beginning to do more in class and his attitude was improving a bit more each day.

During our check-ins, the conversations expanded to other interests, some of his dreams for the future, and other random things. Austin wanted to be a comic book artist or a video game creator. I told him that those sounded like some pretty amazing jobs! I tried to get him to talk about home life and his family. These questions were usually met with a quick change of subject or redirection. Austin was a master of these moves.

I am not sure when things changed or how Austin's guard dropped, but one morning we were having our regular check-in and he seemed a bit down. He initially said that he really did not want to talk about why he was down. Finally, he blurted out that he hates it when his mom calls him 350. I guess he read my face and realized that I didn't understand this reference. Austin then said, my mom calls me 350 because she has told me that she only keeps me around because she gets paid $350 a month in government support for him. Additionally, he said that each time mom gets mad at him, she continues by saying if the money goes away, so do you, 350.

My heart sank and I felt so bad inside. I really didn't now the right thing to say. All I could think to do was to tell him that I thought he was pretty amazing and that it is really important to continue to hope for the future, work hard, and follow your dreams so he can be a comic and video game developer.

The year ended and Austin moved up to the middle school. I periodically checked in on Austin through the middle school principal and the reports were all positive. Austin joined in on several school clubs and activities and the principal's only negative report was about Mom's behavior and lack of involvement.

- What would you have done if you had been in my shoes?
- What role can school play in a situation like this?
- What resources or strategies are there for a student like Austin dealing with this type of home life challenge?
- What role could training in mental health, behavior challenges, and best practices have played in helping these situations?

O.J.

————◆————

As a third-year principal in a building, I had challenged my staff to dig deeper to find students that may be "flying under the radar." In our care team meetings, we usually talked about the same students and if not the same students, it was the same profile of students. Typically, it was a student who was struggling with academics. More times than not it was a student that was having extreme behaviors that prevented him/her from accessing the curriculum. Additionally, their behaviors were interfering with the teacher's ability to teach and the other students' ability to learn. Occasionally, we would discuss a student with poor attendance.

At one of these meeting, the name O.J. was brought up by a teacher. The other teachers responded with puzzled looks. None of them thought there were any issues or reasons to meet about O.J. The teacher that suggested him as someone that should be on our radar, explained that she thought that he really was not connected to anything or anyone at school. She was concerned about his flat affect. We pulled up O.J.'s account in our student information system, but there was nothing that stood out. No discipline referrals, near perfect attendance, and average to above-average grades.

Reluctantly, the other teachers on the team agreed to take some data, do some informal observations, and revisit O.J. at our meeting next month. As things often happen in education, timing is everything. The very next day O.J. moved quickly onto our radar. O.J. inadvertently bumped into another student in the hallway. The other student cursed at him, got in O.J.'s face and pushed him into the wall. Without hesitation, O.J. punched the other student in the face, grabbed him, dropped him to the floor, and continued to punch the other student multiple times until he was pulled off by a school staff member. The other student suffered a concussion and multiple facial injuries.

O.J. was taken to the office. He seemed very calm and showed no facial response. In speaking with him briefly, he was very matter of fact. O.J. was calm, did not seem angry, and surprisingly expressed no remorse.

I called O.J.'s parents. His mom answered and she was quite surprised. She even asked to ensure that I was calling the right parent about the right student. I asked for her to come to school to meet with me and to pick O.J. up.

O.J.'s parents arrived, and we met together with O.J. He point-by-point told them what had happened. O.J.'s description was extremely accurate, since I had pulled up the video and watched it while waiting for his parents. His parents looked shocked and then disappointed. They were speechless and did not say anything to O.J. or ask him any follow-up questions. I asked my assistant principal to sit with him and I asked the parents to come with me. We met for a few minutes and they stressed how surprised they were by his actions and his responses. They apologized for him and asked if they could contact the other student's parents. I let them know that we would convey their feelings to the other student's parents. I then informed them that even though O.J. had a clean record at school, he would have to be suspended for a few days due to the extreme nature of his actions and the harm that he caused the other boy. Not to mention the impact this had on the dozens of students who witnessed this beating. They thanked me and said they completely understood.

O.J.'s parents went with me to his locker to get his belongings. I unlocked his locker and opened the door. In O.J.'s locker we found lots of food, a number of electronic items, random clothing, and other objects that the parents stated did not belong to him.

We returned to the office and asked O.J. about the items and he claimed he had no idea how any of that got in there. I again met separately with the parents before they left and told them that it really seemed as though O.J. was telling the truth. However, this made no sense since it was an individual locker and that nobody else had access to it. After they left, I pulled up video from the previous few days and never saw anyone open O.J.'s locker — except O.J.

When we dug deeper as a team after this event, we found out that O.J. was adopted from an orphanage in Russia as a two-year old.

- – What would you have done if you had been in my shoes?

- – What was going on with O.J.?

- – What tools and strategies could we have used to help O.J. be more successful?

- – What role could training in mental health, behavior challenges, and best practices have played in helping these situations?

Mark

———•———

Mark was a student of mine during my last year of teaching in a gifted academy. He looked like a modern day *Fonzie* from the TV show *Happy Days*. Mark wore a beat-up leather jacket, a white t-shirt, blue jeans, dress shoes, and always had his hair slicked-back. This fashion statement was not the typical fifth-grade attire and he definitely stood out. Mark also stood out because he was about six-feet tall at age ten. In my classroom, there was a particular emphasis on discussions, debates, and presentations. We definitely focused less on reading and writing. This worked out very well for Mark. He was very skilled at critical thinking, problem solving, debating, and thinking on his feet. You could literally ask him a question about anything, and he would respond with a comprehensive and well-articulated answer. I truly believe that to this day that Mark is one of the smartest people I have ever met. I looked forward to Mark coming to the academy on Tuesdays each week. Beyond his intellect, he was polite, funny, and kind.

I received a voice mail message from Mark's home school teacher on a Tuesday morning while I was at arrival duty. She informed me that Mark would not be coming to the academy until further notice. I did not have a moment to call back until lunch break. I called the teacher and she said that she really didn't have time now to talk, but that I could check-in with her after school. I asked if it was all right for me to stop-by and discuss this in person, she agreed and I put a note in my calendar to go to Mark's home school right after school.

I arrived at the home school and the teacher greeted me at the door and walked me to her classroom. She sat down, opened a file, and spread Mark's work all over the table. She stated that Mark is reading at a first-grade level, his handwriting was awful, and his writing more closely matched that of a preschooler. Before I could respond, she stated that last Friday she convinced the principal and Mark's parents to drop him from the gifted academy until he caught up in reading and writing. It was her belief that he would be better suited using the time for an additional reading and writing intervention. For the next fifteen minutes, the teacher spoke about Mark's faults and shared papers and data points that further reinforced his weakness in reading and writing. She also stated that she was shocked to find out that a student like Mark was even in a gifted program.

The last comment was all that I could take. I questioned her about this statement. I asked her if she was familiar with what "Twice Exceptional" means. The teacher said that she had never heard that term before.

I then asked her about any of Mark's strengths, his character, opportunities to capitalize on, etc. The teacher struggled to come up with anything positive to say. I pointed out that she had spent the full fifteen minutes fully focused on Mark's weaknesses. She shrugged her shoulders and said that this was the Mark that she knows and that it is her job to help him catch up.

I spent my fifteen minutes explaining the Mark that I knew. I shared stories about the work that he had completed, the challenging problems that he solved, and also his dreams about changing the world. The teacher responded by saying that she was not aware of any of these items and that she was surprised to hear this about Mark. I asked her if there was anything that I could do to change her mind about Mark coming to the gifted academy. I shared my own personal story, which closely resembled Mark's situation. She stated that she would continue to fight to keep Mark at the home school until he caught up at least a grade level or two in reading and writing.

This tore me apart. I knew how I would have felt if the school had taken away my one day a week that mattered the most to me.

I met with my supervisor and she stated that she was familiar with the situation and that there was nothing we could do at this point. I asked if I could offer to stop-by after school to work with Mark once a week. My supervisor said that it was okay with her if the parents and his home school agreed. Fortunately, they were all on-board.

The first day that I went to the school to work with Mark, I found out that he had been sent home earlier in the day for disrespecting a teacher and breaking school property. I asked if this was a typical behavior, and the school staff stated that he had never had a single discipline referral previously. I tried to reach out to Mark's parents and never heard back. I came back the next week and found out that Mark was out of school for a few days for another similar behavior challenge. I was completely puzzled. I was also puzzled that after multiple attempts, I still had not heard back from Mark's parents. The next week I asked my principal if I could take a personal day to visit Mark at school, or if he was suspended, at home. She said that I could just go and that she would get coverage. I told her that I'd prefer to take the personal day, because one way or another, I would be working with Mark that day.

As I expected, he was not at school. I called all of the contact numbers and left messages stating that I was on my way to their home.

When I arrived, Mark answered the door. The look on his face quickly went from surprise to shame or sadness. I almost didn't recognize him. His hair was disheveled, and he was in shorts and a hoodie. He did not look at all like Fonzie at this point. His mom came to the door as well and she too look surprised. I asked if it would be all right for me to come in and work with Mark. She agreed and apologized for not calling me back. She explained that Mark had been a huge handful at school and at home over the past few weeks. She said that she was at the end of her rope and was thinking about pulling him out of school altogether to home school him.

I went to the kitchen table with Mark and decided that it would be best to jump right into work. I brought information about a pollution challenge in a city that was close to St. Louis. We discussed the challenge and decided together how we would learn more about the specific problem, investigate similar challenges, and come up with some recommendations for how to solve this pollution problem. We then discussed how we would want to present our findings and to whom. He began warming up and I saw the same look of excitement in his eyes (that was absent when I met him at the front door). He was ready to tackle this problem and I was completely convinced that what he would create would be amazing.

Before I left, I asked if we could talk about the behaviors that were occurring at school and at home. Mark agreed and he answered all of my questions. Through this process, he shared that the only positive thing that he had in his schooling was attending the gifted academy. He also went on to say that it is the only time he can be himself and the only time he feels smart. He said that he felt bad about the choices he was making but said that he would rather be suspended from school than to feel and look stupid.

I shared my own story with Mark. He agreed that it was amazing how similar our paths were. I worked with him to find some positives during the school day and a plan for success. I told him that I would actively advocate for him and do anything that I could to help him succeed. I also told him that it was tough for me too, not having him at the academy. He agreed to give the reading and writing interventions a try. Mark said that he would do his best to control his behaviors. I told him that I would see him after school next week to see how things were progressing with the pollution project.

I checked back in with Mark's mom before leaving to discuss the plan. She stated that she would hold-off on the home-schooling plan and would support him returning to the academy if things changed for the better with Mark.

The next morning, I stopped by my supervisor's office to share what the plan was, and she said that she was supportive. I got up and began to walk out of my office. I then stopped and turned around. I asked my supervisor how there could be such a disconnect in the perspectives about the same student. I also asked how someone could know so little about students with high abilities and also learning challenges. She looked up and smiled at me. She then said that it had taken me a few years in the classroom to finally get it. This was going to be an ongoing challenge that I would be facing in my career. Fighting for what is best for students, educating people who don't get it, and learning to flourish in the gray area—to do whatever it takes for students to succeed!

– What would you have done if you had been in my shoes?

– Why did this plan work?

– What other opportunities could there be for students with similar behaviors to Mark?

– What role could training in mental health, behavior challenges, and best practices have played in helping these situations?

Ryan

I first met Ryan during the summer before his Kindergarten school year when his parents brought him to school for a tour. They believed this would help him to adjust. Ryan was a smart little guy who was very enthusiastic about being in "big boy" school.

I met his parents for the second time a few weeks later at Ryan's IEP transition meeting from early childhood to Kindergarten. I learned that there had been significant behavior issues in early childhood. The group worked hard for over two hours and came up with a plan for success. The parents appeared to be on-board and they too were excited for the school year to start.

When the school year did start, things were going very well. I made it a point to check in frequently on Ryan and each time I saw him he told me how great school was and how happy he was to be in "big boy" school. Ryan was a complete rule follower and seemed to adjust very quickly to being in Kindergarten. Ryan's parents also seemed to acclimate quickly to our school. They started volunteering and even joined the PTO board. The teacher implemented a behavior plan and for the most part things went well. Ryan worked hard and exhibited the school's positive character traits.

After winter break, Ryan suddenly began to show some extreme behaviors. He started urinating on himself multiple times a day, he smeared feces all over the bathroom wall, he would run out of the class and hide in different areas of the building, and blow up and overact for no apparent reason. In discussions with Ryan and his parents, they all stated that nothing had changed and there was no clear reason for the change in behaviors. After a few weeks, the behaviors stopped, and Ryan returned to being a model student.

After Spring Break, Ryan missed school on a Monday and Tuesday. The attendance calls went unanswered. This was strange since Ryan had never missed a school day. I was very concerned, so I went with the school resource officer (SRO) to the home to check-in. Ryan answered the door. I asked him where his parents were. He told us that they were still sleeping since they were very tired. The SRO called out Ryan's parents' names and there was no response. The SRO asked that I stay with Ryan as he searched the home. He came back a moment later and whispered in my ear that Ryan's parents were dead in the bedroom. The SRO said that by the look of the room it was a drug overdose. What was more disturbing was that he said it looked like they had been dead for several days.

Further investigating and as a result of Ryan's work with a therapist, it was discovered that when the parents would normally "use" they would leave Ryan with a friend up the street. The friend up the street was on the sex abuse registry and had molested Ryan off and on for several years.

- What can a school do to better detect abuse or molestation?
- What would you have done if you were in my shoes?
- What role could training in mental health, behavior challenges, and best practices have played in helping these situations?

Emily

I was meeting with the district superintendent about staffing for the next year. His secretary knocked on the door and said that I was needed at my school right away because of an issue with a student. My boss told me to go and that we would meet later in the week to finish this meeting. His words and beliefs were always, "kids come first."

I returned to the building and my assistant principal and counselor were at the front door waiting for me. They informed me that they were very worried Emily, a fourth-grade student, was going to harm herself. Emily was an above-average student that had won several attendance and character awards. She generally flew under the radar. She did not seek attention and preferred to work by herself. Emily was the definition of a quiet and compliant student.

Earlier in the day, Emily was not working in class, ignored the teacher's directions, and was not acting like herself. The teacher sent her to the counselor's office. The counselor met individually with her and Emily articulated a detailed plan on how she was going to kill herself after school today. The counselor attempted unsuccessfully to reach out to the parents. She was not able to contact them or the other emergency contacts. The counselor called the assistant principal to discuss what to do and they agreed to call me back to the office from my meeting.

As a team, we decided to call for an ambulance so that Emily would get an emergency psychiatric evaluation. While waiting for the ambulance, I tried to talk to Emily. She had her head down and did not respond. I decided to give her a pen and some paper. I let her know that she could draw or write until the ambulance arrived.

When the paramedics and a police officer arrived, they walked Emily to the ambulance and the counselor went along with them. I let her know that I would finish the school day and then meet them over at the hospital.

We had a school assembly, a parent meeting, and then we finished our dismissal procedures. When the day was over, I returned to my office and began to pack up to head to the hospital. I looked across my office and noticed a folded-up note on the table next to where Emily had been sitting. I thought to myself that this was weird. I generally kept the table cleared off and didn't remember setting anything on it. The folded piece of paper had writing on the outside that said "To Principal P." I unfolded the paper and read the note: "Principal P, I'm sorry for ruining your day and causing such a big problem today. You probably don't know who I am. I am very sad most of the time and alone. My parents don't get me, and every day is pretty much the same. I don't have any friends. I really can't see things getting better in the future. I feel bad and hopeless most of the time. I wonder a lot about whether it is worth being alive at all. Your student, Emily."

I put the note down and started to tear up. I thought about Emily and remembered that she came in third place in our school spelling bee earlier that year; she was the second fastest runner at our annual school run; and, I even remembered the power point that she presented in her class last year about pollution. How could there be such a disconnect between what we knew about Emily and how Emily was feeling right now? I sat there puzzled because in my mind she had everything going for her — she was smart, athletic, and very kind. At the same time, she was only a few hours away from taking her own life before her tenth birthday.

- How do we make sure that everyone is on someone's radar?
- How is your school prepared for students with suicidal thoughts or plans?
- What would you have done if you had been in my shoes?
- What tools and strategies could we have used to help her?
- What role could training in mental health, behavior challenges, and best practices have played in helping these situations?

Marshall

My first encounter with Marshall was during our "Meet the Teacher" event a week before the start of the school year. I remember him being almost as tall as me and he walked up with two younger boys by the hand. All three of them had matching haircuts, similar outfits, and looked like different sized versions of each other. Marshall introduced himself and his two brothers. I asked if they came with anyone else. I was wondering a bit about where his parents were. Marshall told me that they lived in the city and he and his brothers took an hour taxi drive to school. His mom had to stay home with their other younger brothers. Marshall said that it was his job to make sure that his brothers knew who their teachers were and that they were properly introduced. A large group of students and parents approached, and Marshall and his brothers walked down the hallway towards their classes. I thought that this was a bit strange, but I got busy speaking with many other families, and sort of forgot about the encounter.

The next day, I called the counselor to my office to learn more about Marshall and his family. She told me that Marshall was a fifth-grade student who was the man of the house. His father had died when he was a toddler. She also said that to her knowledge there currently was no man living in the home. It was her understanding that Marshall was responsible for getting his brothers ready in the morning. He was the de-facto father. Mom worked a few part-time jobs and usually was sleeping in the morning when the boys left for school.

As the school year started, I learned that Marshall was a popular student and had exceptional manners. This was something that stood out since he called me "sir" at least a dozen times in our brief introductory conversation. Academically, he was a bit below-average but what he lacked in book smarts, he made up in street smarts and emotional intelligence. The school staff members really liked him and he smiled a lot and seemed to remember everything. They all envisioned a bright future for him in a relationship business.

On a Tuesday afternoon, Marshall was brought to the office by the recess monitor. I immediately thought that this must have been to brag on Marshall's behavior or for a character sticker for model behavior. Marshall's face told another story. He did not make eye contact and sat with his head in his hands. The recess monitor said that he apparently started screaming at another student and pushed him to the ground. This appeared to be completely unprovoked. It was also very out of character for Marshall. To say that I was a bit surprised would have been a huge understatement.

Marshall did not respond immediately to my questions. This was unusual behavior for Marshall as well. After a while, he finally sat up, looked at me, and said that he was ready to answer any questions. He admitted that the behaviors were all his fault and that the other student did not do anything to provoke him. The other boy was just at the wrong place at the wrong time. Marshall said that he had to man-up and that he was ready to accept any consequence that he received.

I told him that I could not understand at all what had happened and why. After a series of other questions, Marshall stated that his family was thrown out of their apartment for not paying rent. They spent the last few nights sleeping in his mom's car. Marshall said that his mom was crying and told him that she had no idea what they were going to do. He said that he thought this was partly his fault because as the man of the house he should have been able to do something about this. He started to cry and put his head back down.

- What can the school do to help Marshall and his family?
- What would you have done if you had been in my shoes?
- What tools and strategies could we have used to help him be more successful?
- What role could training in mental health, behavior challenges, and best practices have played in helping these situations?

Scott

———◆———

One of my goals as a principal was to attend all of our Individualized Education Plan (IEP) meetings. I never fully achieved this goal, due to emergencies and scheduling conflicts, but I did attend several hundred of these meetings during my education career. One of these IEP meetings really stood out to me and is one that I have not forgotten.

The meeting was for a fifth-grade student named Scott. Scott had four siblings. Scott and his siblings were all on extensive IEP's for academics and behaviors. As a family, it seemed as though a day did not go by without one of them being sent to the office. The behaviors were all related to disrupting the learning of others, sleeping at school, stealing food from other students, and other poor choices. Conversations, consequences, and other strategies were generally unsuccessful.

The IEP meeting had been scheduled and rescheduled a number of times due to conflicts with Scott's mom's schedule. As a group, we decided to see if we could conduct the meeting at their home. Our hope was that this would remove a major and ongoing challenge which was a lack of childcare and unreliable transportation.

Additionally, she refused to take a taxi and did not want to conduct this meeting by phone.

In preparing for the meeting, the consensus was that Scott's mom had always appeared supportive of the school. Members of the team stated that it was their belief that she made them do their homework and if they ever got in trouble she enforced the school consequences at home.

When the team arrived at the home, Scott's mom welcomed them at the door. She stated that she had spent the past few days cleaning up so that the home was presentable. I right away noticed that there were four mattresses on the floor in the living room, bugs were crawling all over the wall, piles of dog feces were scattered across the floor, there was a giant hole in the roof (that you could see the sun through), dirty dishes stacked in the sink, and bags of trash were covering most of the floor.

Once everyone sat down on chairs and the sofa, Mom must have recognized the expressions on the guests' faces. She stated that she was doing the best that she could. School staff tried to steer the conversation in a different direction and asked that we start the IEP meeting. We all tried to start with questions that would produce positive answers before digging into the tougher questions. They asked about the activities that the family enjoyed participating in. Mom really couldn't share any that stood out aside from watching TV together. She told the school staff that the kids rarely went outside due to the neighborhood being very dangerous and the illegal activities that occurred at the closest park.

Many of our IEP related questions were not immediately answered by Scott's mom. She stared at us and looked as though she did not understand the language that we were speaking. On several occasions, I tried to translate the IEP language into simpler words. This really did not help much. Mom asked many times for us to repeat the question or to explain what we meant. She said that she dropped out of school when she was sixteen. Mom said that she dropped out partly because she was pregnant with Scott. She also said that at that time in her life, she was failing most of her classes and that she hated being in the special classes because it made her feel stupid. She said that she wasn't stupid, she just had to take a lot of medicine to control her mood. Mom also said that it is really hard for her to help her kids with their homework, because it was too hard for her.

- What does this family need right now?
- What can you do when mom appears to be doing the best that she knows how to do?
- What would you have done if you had been in my shoes?
- What tools and strategies could we have used to help him be more successful?
- What role could training in mental health, behavior challenges, and best practices have played in helping these situations?

Jay

-----◆-----

I was introduced to Jay when I was touring an elementary school building during an interview process for a principal position. He was in the self-contained classroom for students with behavior challenges. I remembered him because he had a huge smile and because he told me his name about twenty times in the few minutes that I was visiting the room. He also asked if I could be his best friend.

I ended up being offered the position to become the principal and on the first day of school, Jay re-introduced himself to me at morning arrival duty. He also asked if I had decided on whether or not I would be his best friend. I told him that of course we were "BFF's."

Jay was a second-grade student. He resided about forty-five minutes from our school. Jay lived with his mom and several siblings and they were poor—Mom was between jobs. The family did not own a car and relied on public transportation to get around. Jay came to our district with an IEP for behaviors and academics. He had a big smile and most of the time a positive attitude. Whenever he felt like he was unsuccessful or if he made a mistake, he would completely change. The big smile and positive attitude would be replaced with an angry face and rage. He became aggressive and unpredictable. At these times, he would not respond to adults and it took him a long time to get out of this state. I remember having to dig very deep in my toolbox and bag of tricks to try to deescalate my best friend, Jay.

One morning, I was in my office preparing for a before school staff meeting. I received a call from our transportation director. She said that there had been an incident on the bus and that the police were heading to the scene. I was really worried it had been an accident with another vehicle, but the transportation director told me there was no accident, just a behavior incident with a student. I left school right away.

When I arrived at the location of the incident, the police were in the process of handcuffing Jay and forcibly removing him from the bus. This was not a very positive visual, since Jay was about two feet shorter than the officers and the handcuffs were at least a few sizes too big for him.

The officers informed me that Jay had threatened another student with a weapon and they had been instructed to take him to the police station. One of the officers made it a point to tell me that it doesn't matter how young or small a person is, a threat is a threat and that it has to be taken very seriously. I immediately contacted Jay's mom and followed the police car to the station. Jay was released to his mother a few hours after arriving there. A juvenile court date was set, and Jay's mom took him home.

After meeting with the bus driver, speaking with students, and reviewing the video from the bus recording, I had a pretty good idea of what had happened. Apparently, another student told Jay that he was dumb and his mom was stupid and fat. The other student picked the wrong words with the wrong second grade student, as these were major triggers for Jay. It took very little time for Jay to get upset and escalate. He threatened to cut the other student with his scissors. Jay pulled out scissors from his bag and began waving them around and aiming them at the other student. The bus driver immediately pulled the bus off of the highway and called the police and the transportation director.

When I got back to my office, my secretary told me that my supervisor wanted to meet with me immediately. I went to his office and he closed the door. He said that he had heard about the situation on the bus. News like this travels like wildfire in a school district.

Before I could say anything, he told me that this student would need to be suspended from school for ten days with a recommendation for the board to extend this to a month or longer. He then said that this student would never be permitted to take the bus to our school. I pointed out that this would have the same effect as if we expelled him, since Jay's family would have no way of getting to our school. He would have to attend a school near his home which didn't have the same resources we did to support him. My supervisor nodded and said that this would work out well because it would remove a dangerous student from our community. I told him that we certainly don't want anyone to be hurt, but the scissors Jay used were made of plastic and were not sharp at all. I also stressed that Jay had made some real progress this year and that he has a real future if we can continue to help him with his behaviors and his learning challenges. My supervisor told me that his decision was made, and nothing was going to change his mind. I turned around feeling both frustrated and disappointed. I knew that we had failed this student. Worst of all, I was helpless to do anything to change this situation.

I reached out to Jay's mom and told her about the suspension and about Jay losing bus privileges. She pleaded with me to reconsider. I could hear that she was crying. By the end of the conversation, she said that she understood and thanked me for everything we had done to help her son. She stressed that there would be no way for him to get to school and that he would have to enroll elsewhere. I really was not able to think of anything to say. She then asked about his belongings in the classroom. I told her that I would gather them and drop them off at their home after school today.

When I arrived at their home, Jay met me at the door. He said that he was sorry for what he had done. He looked me in the eyes and said that surely, I knew he would never hurt another student with scissors or any other object. I nodded and said nothing. He thanked me for bringing his belongings and as I turned to leave, he ran down the stairs after me. Jay gave me a big hug and said that he hoped we could still be best friends.

On my ride home, I could not get Jay's face out of my mind. I felt like the system had failed him and that I didn't and couldn't do a damn thing about it. To this day, I still think about Jay. I wonder how I would have handled this situation differently, if I had been the supervisor. I struggled with balancing school safety versus helping a student. I knew that if I was given the chance, we could help Jay and completely change his life trajectory. My head said one thing and my heart was screaming out a different message.

- What would you have done if you had been in my shoes?
- What tools and strategies could we have used to help him be more successful?
- What role could training in mental health, behavior challenges, and best practices have played in helping these situations?

Albert

————— ✦ —————

A lbert was a very small fourth grade student. I met him during the summer before the school year started. I was moving some things into my office and I saw him shooting hoops by himself on our playground. He approached me and asked if I was the new assistant principal. I introduced myself and shook his hand. He then asked if I would play HORSE with him. I thought about the long list of things that I had to get done and how far behind I was already, but I quickly decided that HORSE with a student trumped everything on that list. While playing basketball, he asked me several questions and literally spoke for twenty minutes straight without taking a breath. He was funny, interesting, and seemed very intelligent. When we finished playing, he thanked me for spending the time with him and he walked home. I went back in the building and started to tackle the many items that were on my long list of things to accomplish.

A few weeks later we had some back to school IEP meetings. One of them was for a student named Albert. I pulled the file so that I would be prepared for the meeting. To my surprise, this was the same Albert that I played basketball with a few weeks prior. He had a list of a dozen school suspensions, at least six DSM diagnosis listed, and was assigned to the self-contained classroom for eighty-five percent of the day. Something did not add up. The parents did not show up for the meeting but gave verbal permission to conduct the meeting in their absence. This was the first IEP that I had ever attended where there was not one positive word spoken about this student. Even when they asked for any strengths, nobody around the table could share any. I spoke up and said that based on my twenty-minute encounter with him I felt he had several strengths: a good outside jump shot, excellent communications skills, an inquisitive nature, and a big smile. I looked around the table and everyone stared at me like I was either crazy or talking about another student.

The school year started with a bang from Albert. He became upset in class and ran down the hall and straight out of the building towards his home. I managed to catch-up to him before he crossed a major street and I convinced him to walk back to the school and into my office. Albert was crying and obviously frustrated. He said that everyone in the school was mean to him and that they all thought he was a bad kid. In my head, I thought that he was exactly right— certainly based on the IEP meeting participants. We had a nice talk and Albert seemed to calm down. I asked if he would like to join me outside for a game of HORSE. He gave me a strange look, but then said, "Are you sure?" I told him definitely and he enthusiastically agreed to play.

Once we were outside, Albert asked if he was going to be suspended. I told him that we would forget about this one, but that if there was a next one, he would be sent home. We discussed some better choices for next time, as running out of the room and building was a real safety issue. I stressed that I wanted him to be safe, because I liked him, cared about him, and did not want anything to happen to the school's best basketball player. He smiled at me and asked if it would be okay if he could come to my office when he got upset, instead of running out of the building. I told him that was a great idea. We played basketball for about ten minutes and decided that it was time to go back inside to prepare for lunch time. Albert turned his head, looked me in the eyes and said that this was the nicest thing that anyone at school had ever done for him.

Albert kept to his word. There were several other times that he got upset and frustrated, but instead of running out of the building, he ran to my office, sat in a corner, and cooled off. Each time it would take about ten minutes before he was ready to talk and process what happened. Albert never got suspended that year and staff regularly shared some positives about him. Amazing what one small act of kindness can do to help a student be successful.

- How can we encourage others to change the ways that we think about and speak about a student?
- What do you do when there are a hundred negatives and no positive about a student?

- Why did HORSE and the cool-off office work for Albert?

- What would you have done if you had been in my shoes?

- What tools and strategies could we have used to help him be more successful?

- What role could training in mental health, behavior challenges, and best practices have played in helping these situations?

Jenny

———————◆———————

Jenny was a high-school student at our school. She was very active in just about every school activity possible. She was involved in school plays, athletic teams, and the honor society. My first impression of Jenny was that she was going places. She was positive, kind, a hard worker, and a good friend to many students. In staff meetings, Jenny was often the student that was recommended for a student leadership position or activity. I had never heard a negative word about her.

In the middle of her Junior year, Jenny slowly started to reduce her participation in school related activities. Her attendance at school and her grades began to decline. This happened over the course of several weeks, but we did not immediately notice this since it was around the holiday season.

After winter break, Jenny missed a few consecutive days. Since there were many students who went on prolonged holiday vacations, this did not raise a red flag. She returned to school for two days and then it was the weekend. On Monday, Jenny was not at school. It was on my list to reach out to the family to see what was going on with Jenny.

I was heading back to school from an off-site principal's meeting. I had to stop at the local gas station to fill up my tank. While the gas was pumping, I went inside to grab a sandwich and a diet soda. As I was waiting in line to check-out, I did a double-take and noticed that Jenny was working the register. When it was my turn to pay, Jenny looked up and the color ran out of her face. She said absolutely nothing. I paid for my items and asked her if she was okay. She nodded and looked down. I asked her to come see me before school tomorrow.

Jenny showed up early for school and knocked on my office door. Before I could say anything, she sat down in a chair and started crying. She told me that her dad had a fight with her mom and left. The family had not seen him in nearly two months. This situation really hit her mom hard. She had not showered or left the apartment in weeks. Jenny went on to say that she had to get a job, or they would be thrown out of the apartment. Unfortunately, the only shift that was available for her was during the school day. Jenny said that she really missed seeing her friends and was very sad that she has had to give up so many of the things she loved to do. Jenny looked up and through the tears said, "What else am I supposed to do?".

I asked if there was anything we could do to help. She shrugged her shoulders. I told her I would get with the school social worker and counselor to research some resources to assist her family.

- How do you balance survival needs with school rules and policies?

- What resources are there available for families that are in crisis?

- What would you have done if you had been in my shoes?

- What tools and strategies could we have used to help her be more successful?

- What role could training in mental health, behavior challenges, and best practices have played in helping these situations?

Ollie

———•———

Ollie was a ten-year-old dream student! He was enthusiastic, positive, kind-hearted, and enjoyed learning. Ollie was the definition of a "teacher's helper." I remember four teachers fighting to get him on their class roster for the next school year. He displayed all of the ideal character traits that we encouraged students to exhibit and was an ambassador for the school (meaning he gave tours to visitors). I received many compliments from our school visitors about how Ollie was charismatic, funny, and outgoing.

I first met Ollie when I was an assistant principal on lunch and recess duty. I noticed that Ollie made rounds during these social times. He appeared to make it a point to play with all of the kids at recess, especially the ones that were alone. I also recalled him asking me on many occasions if it was okay if he moved to another table to sit with the student who was eating alone in the lunchroom. Each year Ollie was recognized for citizenship and for his grades.

One morning the school buses began to arrive to our school. The third bus pulled up and Ollie ran right past all of us into the building. He did not greet anyone. Once inside, he ran through the hallways bumping into kids and appearing completely out of control. While running through the hall, he ended up knocking over a large antique glass display case. This shattered into many pieces and startled everyone in that area. Ollie got up and kept running. I cut through the library and managed to block his path. I guided him into my office, but Ollie would not make eye contact and looked completely out of sorts. He was breathing quickly, was pale, and appeared as though his engine was running on overdrive. He did not respond to any of my questions and sat down on the floor in the fetal position and rocked back and forth for about twenty minutes. This was definitely not the Ollie that I knew.

Eventually, Ollie looked at me and began to cry. I asked him what was wrong. He glanced up and said, "There was a dead body at my bus-stop this morning. There was blood everywhere. I didn't know what to do. I heard a gunshot last night—it woke me up. This must have been the person who was shot. I don't think I'm going to be able to get this out of my mind."

- How do you deal with a student that is acting completely out of character?
- What does Ollie need right now and what will he need moving forward?
- How is your school and staff prepared to handle a situation like this one?
- What would you have done if you had been in my shoes?

- What tools and strategies could we have used to help him be more successful?

- What role could training in mental health, behavior challenges, and best practices have played in helping these situations?

Simone

As a fifth-grade teacher in a gifted academy, I met many exceptional students. By definition, all of my students were gifted, talented, and high potential individuals. They spent one day a week at our academy and four days at their home schools. So many of my former students have gone on to Ivy League schools and other highly competitive universities. Several are now in successful careers—lawyers, doctors, scientists, entrepreneurs, educators, etc.

Of the hundreds of students that I taught, one stands out to me. Her name was Simone. She was extremely intelligent, popular, and kind to her classmates. Even in a room full of gifted students, she was on a whole different level. She had a gift of learning things quickly and permanently. It seemed as though she could turn a one-time exposure into lifelong knowledge and quick application. The interesting thing about Simone was that even though she was highly-gifted, she was also very personable. Additionally, she spoke with normal words and never flaunted her intelligence.

Outside of school, Simone was involved in junior pageants, church youth group, sports teams, community organizations, theater groups, and other activities. On one occasion, I remember her asking me when her student-led parent/teacher conference was. I told her and she opened her planner to write this in the book. I noticed that her planner was very colorful and well-organized. I also noticed that there were no empty boxes. I asked her about her schedule, and she said that she loved being involved in so many things and that she liked staying busy. This made her happy.

On the conference night, her parents came without Simone. I greeted them and told them to have a seat. I then asked where Simone was. They said that she was "struggling with math" (she received a ninety-nine on an advanced math test), so she had to do a double-session with her math tutor. Her parents apologized for her absence and we discussed her progress and I shared the many positives. Her parents asked a few questions and I answered these questions enthusiastically. Simone's parents seemed satisfied and as they stood up to leave, they said that due to her great performance at the academy, they were going to allocate an extra hour of sleep for her on Sunday. This statement went over my head and did not resonate. I moved on to another conference and forgot about their comment.

The next week Simone came to class in the morning and apologized for missing the conference. On the way to art class, I asked her to hang back for a minute. She complied and asked if she was in trouble. I told her that I just had some questions for her. I was very curious, and a bit concerned about her busy schedule. She shared that her parents wake her up at 5:00 am each day, including weekends, and that she is allowed to go to sleep when all of her activities, homework, and chores are finished. When I asked her about this, she said that this was generally between 11:00 pm and midnight. As I was looking at her, the expression on her face quickly and completely changed. She appeared to be in major distress. Before I could ask any other questions, she started to cry and yelled out, "Mr. Pearlman, I am so tired all the time. Please help me!" I felt so badly for her. I walked with her to get a drink of water and to splash some water on her face. After a few minutes, I asked if she was up for art class. She stated that she would be fine. As soon as I dropped her off, I moved very quickly to the counselor's office. I filled the counselor in on what had happened and she asked to meet with Simone right after art class.

After her meeting with Simone, the counselor checked back with me and said that she was very concerned about Simone. Apparently, beyond not sleeping, she was not eating, and she was having thoughts about harming herself. The counselor called the parents in and connected them with an outside therapist and psychiatrist.

- How do you help encourage students and their parents to find balance?

- How do you locate students that are struggling with emotions, pressure, and other stress—when they are not obvious or easy to find?

- What would you have done if you had been in my shoes?

- What tools and strategies could we have used to help her be more successful?

- What role could training in mental health, behavior challenges, and best practices have played in helping these situations?

Case Studies
Wrap-Up

---◆---

You just read about several students. I wonder if any of these students sound like those that you have encountered in the past or those that you are currently working with in your school or district. They were selected because they represent many mental health, behavior-related concerns, or situations that occur in children and teens all across the country.

The student stories were also selected as some examples of positive successes, some as negative outcomes, and others that I wish we could have a re-do on. My hope is that you can learn from our successes, our failures, and other challenges that we encountered.

I think it is really important to understand that we all did and do the best that we can with the information that is available and with the skills and tools that we have at a particular point in time. This is why

I encourage friends, colleagues, and others to work together in problem solving and to share what you know with others. I also believe that is essential that we continue to seek and acquire more knowledge.

Did you find it challenging to answer the questions at the end of the case study? As your role in school changes and/or as you have more experience, do you envision your answers changing? How would others in your school answer the question and/or react to the stories?

What do you need now to help you when encountering students like those discussed in this book? How can I help?

During this process and in your own real-life situations, do your heart and head handle the situations differently? If so, how do you make the "right" decision?

SHOCKERS
Approach

---◆---

In schools and districts across the country, there is one constant in all of them. The use of acronyms. I decided that since we are all familiar with acronyms, why not include another that will hopefully be easy to remember in helping to support students that are struggling. The approach that I will describe works for those dealing with challenging behaviors, trauma, academics, or in many other ways. It is the "SHOCKERS Approach." I developed this concept about five years ago. This is a process and approach that I regularly update and improve.

SHOCKERS stands for:

Schoolwide team

Hope

Out of the box thinking

Critical friend (captain of the team)

Kindness

Empathy

Response to intervention

Self-care (to combat stress and secondary trauma)

I have used the SHOCKERS approach with hundreds of students and have shared this when training thousands of educators all over the country. Let's break down each of the components in SHOCKERS.

Schoolwide team:

Students who are struggling need a schoolwide team. This is so important because we can draw on the knowledge, background, and strengths of many caring and skilled educators. In this process, ensure that you bring together a large enough group so there is the opportunity for the development of many ideas and diversity of thought. The group works to create strategies for success. The strategies and methods are developed into SMART goals (another "s" word). By using the SMART acronym, we ensure our goals are specific, measurable, attainable, realistic, and timely. Effective schools have a schoolwide team ready to act to support a student that is struggling. Another important item is that everyone on this team has a voice and speaking rights at the table. I worked hard to ensure that I was never the smartest person at the table. I also worked to make sure that I developed a culture that did not have "yes" men/women. Some of the best ideas and strategies, and those most outside of the box, were developed by unconventional members of the team. A good example of this was an amazing reading intervention that was developed by our math specialist who claimed to have never taught anyone to read in his life. If you are developing this group from scratch, make sure to dedicate time to develop norms and protocols. Every minute invested in this process will pay back hours in efficiency and productivity.

Hope:

Students who are struggling need hope that tomorrow will be better than today! Otherwise, why is it worth getting up in the morning and coming to school to fail?

While co-leading a training, a therapist colleague of mine said that the number one reason people attempt suicide is hopelessness. Hope is such a powerful tool. It is critical to teach our students to have hope for the future. We do this by helping them dream big and then including supports and scaffolding for them to achieve goals that lead them to their big dream. It is also important to celebrate successes, no matter how small.

In my career, it was always very important for me to help students get a quick-win. Even the smallest success can help someone continue to push through a challenging situation and to continue to hope for the future. For students, especially those in difficult home situations, hope is so important. They need to know that their current circumstance is not permanent and that there is a way out. I spent a lot of time reflecting on those people that survived horrible situations and those that did not. I think about those who survived the holocaust. How did someone have hope for the future when they were starving, sick, beaten, and witnesses to the killing of millions of their friends and family? The quote from Elie Wiesel, "Even in darkness it is possible to create light," seems to illustrate the power of hope. I think about the miners that were stuck underground for weeks in darkness, without adequate rations, and quickly running out of oxygen. Somehow these individuals had hope and kept their faith. I believe this is the power of hope and something that needs to be taught, built up, and supported in our students.

Out of the box thinking:

"In order to attain the impossible, one must attempt the absurd." – Miguel de Cervantes

I had about twenty-five students that were hijacking our school. They were popular and they were leading by making bad choices. Each of these students in their own way were disrupting their own learning and the learning of others. These students represented ninety-five percent of our discipline referrals. Loss of recess, lunch in the office, loss of bus privileges, missing school parties, in-school suspensions, and out-of-school suspensions did not work. I truly felt that we had tried just about everything.

I attended a mixed martial arts event (MMA) with my son, who was doing the play-by-play. As I was standing against the back wall thinking about my group of twenty-five students, a former MMA fighter, current gym owner, and friend tapped me on the back. He said that this was the first time he had seen me without a smile on my face. He asked, "What gives, dude?" I told him that I had students that were ruining my school and I was at the bottom of the barrel and out of ideas for what to do. We spoke for a while about our own experiences in school. We laughed and agreed that if we attended this school, we probably both would have been part of the group of twenty-five. He asked me about what would have helped me at that age. I told him it would have been something way out of the box and something that would engage me in a fun real world activity. I also said that it would have needed to be something that involved a positive role model. In that moment, it seemed like magic because we both said that we should do a morning martial arts program for the students.

In the back of the arena, my friend and I sketched out our plan on a dirty napkin with a broken pencil (sometimes the best ideas are on a dirty napkin). He agreed to volunteer once a week in the morning to help. He would teach Brazilian Jiu-Jitsu (ground martial arts with submission) and I would teach stand-up boxing. (My dad taught me boxing when I was a kid, since he had boxed in his youth.)

I immediately pitched the idea to my supervisor. He was a huge fight sports fan, so he was very supportive. I also wrote a resignation letter and told him that if someone got hurt or something went wrong, I would own it and resign. He laughed and said he thought the letter was unnecessary. The group started and after a few minor hiccups, it turned out to be a huge success. We built a family and team. Each member of the group of twenty-five felt responsible to each other. Nobody wanted to let their teammates down. We recorded data, held ourselves accountable, infused positive leadership messages, and had a lot of fun. Of the group, twenty-four of the twenty-five students improved in achievement, attendance, and attitude. The number of office referrals and suspended days reduced by ninety-eight percent for the group.

This idea was just one example of an out of the box strategy. Your school doesn't need to start a martial arts group, but you can do something. The more out of the box, the better for your students that are struggling the most. In other years, we added a movement intervention for students that were too high, too low, needed sensory input, or just needed to get their wiggles out. This too was out of the box, required help from the team, and became a success as well. These students arrived at their class ready to learn and the teacher had their other students off and running and were ready to receive the students from movement.

Truly, the what is less important than the why. Just do something and keep trying. The struggling students, the non-struggling students, and the staff deserve it!

<u>C</u>ritical friend:

*"A mentor is someone who allows you to see the
hope inside yourself." – Oprah Winfrey*

A critical friend is someone that looks out for a student. It is someone that ensures they are on someone's radar. This is someone that won't let a student fail. A critical friend can be a teacher, administrator, counselor, SRO, cafeteria worker, neighbor, school volunteer, or anybody that is in a student's life. I was told once that there was a sociological study which looked at successful professionals (doctors, judges, teachers, nurses, etc.) who when growing up were in the highest risk category. These were individuals that would have had very high numbers of Adverse Childhood Experiences (ACEs). The researchers would have predicted this group to have had a high risk of joining gangs, dropping out of school, being incarcerated, having an addiction, and potentially deceased before age twenty-one. But, somehow, the group of successful professionals made it out of this high-risk situation. This puzzled the researchers. When doing a deep analysis and many interviews, the researchers found that the one constant in all of these people was that they had a critical friend. This could be nothing more than a daily check-in, but the critical friend was someone that cared about the individual, helped them have hope for the future, and was there to support them along the way. You can't be this for everyone, but you can for at least one student. You can change their life trajectory and you may even save a life! This can be done in as little as thirty seconds twice a day.

My critical friend was Mrs. Rivers in high school. I remember struggling greatly with writing as I went through my K-12 education career. As I mentioned previously, I'm sure that I had an undiagnosed learning disability in this area. I had Mrs. Rivers in my senior year of high-school. She was a tough veteran teacher that was someone you did not want to mess with (she was a bit scary). The school year was ending, and my thoughts were on going to parties, hanging out with friends, and preparing to leave for college. Mrs. Rivers' class was the only one without a final. Her class required a ten-page paper to finish the class. I was happy that my paper was done, and I had turned it in. Admittedly, it was not a well-written paper. I wrote fast and did not put much thought into it. I figured I could cruise right through the last class on the last day of school. The class finished and I'm sure I jumped up and was mid-sprint heading to the door when Mrs. Rivers cut off my path and asked that I stay after for a minute to speak with her. Naively, I thought she wanted to wish me well for going off to college. This was definitely not the reason for staying after class. She said that my paper was not very good and that she thought I could do much better. She said that she would like for me to re-write this and turn it in on Monday.

Somehow, I reached deep down and came up with the courage to tell her that I was not interested in re-writing the paper. I also told her that

I did the math. I calculated that I could get an F on the paper and still have a passing grade in her class. I then said that I was accepted into college and had sufficient grades to move on and forget about this place. She agreed that I would still earn a D but pointed out that she was prepared to give me an I (incomplete). With a smirk on her face, she asked if I would be able to graduate and go to college with an "I" in a credit class. It felt like I'd been punched in the gut. I thought for a second. She was right. I questioned her and asked if she would really do this. She said that she definitely would.

I went home that night, re-wrote the paper, and came to meet with her on Monday. She reviewed my paper and told me that it was still not good enough. She insisted that I re-write it again and come back the next day. I was very upset about this. But what choice did I have?

This back and forth with Mrs. Rivers went on for several days. I tried to get my parents involved and pleaded with Mrs. Rivers. I pointed out that graduation was only a few days away, but she marked up the paper each time with suggestions and a big "I" to remind me that it was still incomplete.

Finally, after several attempts, Mrs. Rivers reviewed my paper and said it was a complete paper. She agreed to change my grade and allow me to move on. I left pissed off and upset. What a terrible way to start the summer! I was stressed the whole time that my parents would kill me if I walked through graduation with an empty degree container. I worried during the process that I wouldn't start college on time. But mostly, I kept going back to how awful this experience had been and how it was such an inconvenience. I wanted to complain the principal and tell him that I was singled out unfairly. Ultimately, I decided to let it go and forget about Mrs. Rivers.

A few years after I graduated from college, I ran into one of my high-school principals. I'm not sure why I decided to share my repeated paper writing story with him and asked if he had been aware of the terrible way that I finished my high-school experience with Mrs. Rivers. He said that Mrs. Rivers had retired about five years ago and passed away in the last year. He said that he remembered how Mrs. Rivers persuaded him to allow her to "push Pearlman." I must have looked puzzled because he said that he kept telling her to let it go, to just pass him, and let him get on with his life. She fought him though and stated that this would be a great life lesson for this student and that he would be better for it. The principal then asked me if I was aware that Mrs. Rivers didn't have a car and took a taxi to work every day—about a thirty-minute ride each way. Those days that she came in to meet with me were on her nickel. She wasn't paid for that time and it probably cost her about a hundred dollars.

None of this information had immediately clicked in my brain. I had this situation and memory all wrong. Mrs. Rivers was my critical friend. She would not let me fail, she had faith in my ability, and she wanted only the best for me. I felt terrible thinking about this and how

I had felt about her at the time. I promised myself that I would work very hard to be like Mrs. Rivers to other students. There really is so much power in a critical friend.

Kindness:

"No act of kindness, no matter how small, is ever wasted." – Aesop

An important attribute in a successful educator is kindness. The simple act of kindness can positively change a student's day. These acts of kindness over time can change a student's life. Kindness is particularly important for struggling students when even the smallest amount of kindness is critical because it is possible that this is the only positive and kind act that a student gets in their life. Another important benefit of kindness is that it has been scientifically proven to cause more kindness. Kindness is believed to spread like a virus. Being kind is also a positive for the person who performs the act. Brain researchers talk about the endorphins that are released when performing a kind act.

I probably experienced a "helper's high," which is what Melanie Rudd, an assistant professor of marketing at the University of Houston, calls the boost we get from being kind. Much of Rudd's research into understanding what makes us happy has focused on this aspect of giving, which she calls "impure altruism." The "act of helping others and seeing others happy . . . gives us this warm glow," she says, which benefits us (Petrow, 2018).

I recently ran into a former student of mine at the grocery store. Bailey was in fifth grade when I was her teacher about fourteen years ago. She is now a teacher at a local elementary school. Bailey gave me a hug and asked if I remembered her from school. I did remember her right away. I truly never forget a face. She obviously looked older than I remembered her and she was much taller and now wore glasses. Bailey told me that she owed me a huge thank you. At that moment, I really could not think of why she would be thanking me, so I asked her why. She said that I was always very kind to her in a million little ways. I asked her to give some examples of what she remembered. She said that I bought her lunch when she had no money in her account; I helped her find her mood ring when she lost it on the playground; I treated her like a real person, and not just a kid; I asked her about her hopes and dreams, and she knew that I definitely believed in her.

Bailey also informed me that fifth grade was a very challenging time in her life. Her parents divorced and she didn't get to see much of her dad. It was great to have a positive male in her life. This obviously made me feel good, but I really didn't think that I treated her any differently than anyone else. She then told me that she always wanted to be a teacher just like Mr. Pearlman. I guess the message here is that the little acts of kindness can go a long way for helping students to become kind and caring people (and in some cases, other kind and caring teachers). The most important part is that these acts of kindness didn't require very much, didn't cost much, and made a huge impact on another person's life.

Empathy:

The more a challenging student's behavior rises, so must our empathy. Empathy is very simply trying to put yourself in someone else's shoes. It is so important to try and understand where a student is coming from and what they need at that time.

Over the years, when I hired teachers, I worked very hard in the interview process to ask questions that would gauge the candidate's empathy. Once, I "inherited" a teacher that had very good results on the state high stakes test. Unfortunately, I could find no evidence of empathy in this individual. There were so many situations that occurred that further demonstrated her lack of empathy. This was very challenging since she was a third-grade teacher.

One particular situation with this teacher stands out to me. She came to my office to ask if any new students could go right away to their specials class and then she could meet them later. The rationale was because this cut into her plan time and that was not fair (in her opinion). I thought about the few new kids that arrived to her class after the school year started. All of them had challenging home lives, had recently experienced trauma, and literally had moved to town only a day or two earlier. These students desperately needed love, kindness, compassion, and a connection. Unfortunately, these were of a secondary concern for this teacher, because her needs were apparently more important. No matter how many times I discussed this and the importance of empathy with this teacher, she never got it. I spoke with my supervisor later in the year about this teacher and her lack of empathy. His response was that it is all about results. I argued that this may be the case in secondary buildings, but not in my elementary school. I offered to transfer her to any of the other building for any other teacher that was available. My only request was that the next teacher had to have at least a morsel of empathy.

Part of the trainings that I do, have real-world scenarios that force people to put themselves in another person's shoes. In many cases, this causes people to cry, to feel, and to come up with strategies that can support the student. This is a great exercise in remembering to think of the other person and their needs. Additionally, this is a starting point to build empathy. For some people, empathy is natural an innate. For other people, it is something that needs to be developed. To this day, I still can't think of a more important trait for a teacher!

Response to intervention (RTI):

When I started in education, most people had never heard of response to intervention (RTI). After a while, RTI became synonymous with progress monitoring for reading. With time this grew to math. I attribute a lot of this growth in use and understanding to the *AIMSweb* progress monitoring program (and other similar tools). At the time, I wondered why RTI couldn't be used for all areas with students of different concerns, abilities, and challenges. This process is completely applicable to struggling students in academics, behaviors, and other areas. The secret sauce behind RTI really is not that secret, difficult, or unique. The elements to implementing this in the areas of struggling students include: determining the skill deficiency, locating intervention tool(s) to focus on deficient skill, implementing with fidelity, monitoring progress, allowing some time, and evaluating progress. If successful, keep implementing the intervention, and if possible, increase intensity. If unsuccessful, tweak intervention and try again. If repeatedly unsuccessful, gather a group to brainstorm and determine next step(s). I want to stress that a great intervention may not work the first time or two. Conversely, a lousy intervention may work the first or second time.

If your school is not currently using an RTI process for behaviors, today is a great day to start!

Self-care (to combat stress and secondary trauma):

The most important and most rewarding job is that of an educator. As amazing as this career and calling is, it can also cause a high-level of stress. Additionally, in dealing with students that have been traumatized, there is a high risk of secondary trauma for the teacher.

A recent addition to my trainings is how to make teacher self-care a well-utilized practice and finding a way for this to fit into a busy person's schedule. There are so many resources that discuss the different types of self-care strategies. You can access these by doing a google search on "self-care", "teacher self-care" or "mindfulness." A very simple example of one is ensuring that you take some time each day (even a few minutes) for yourself. This can be listening to music, doing some deep-breathing, or even a short walk on a beautiful day. For self-care to be successful in a school, there has to be a commitment to checking-in and monitoring your neighbor or colleague. Perhaps the most successful model, is to have a "self-care buddy." This daily activity can be done in a few minutes each day. One year, a grade-level team in my building started having their daily team meetings while walking the track together. This was a win-win.

When thinking about self-care, I think about the instructions on an airplane for when the pressure changes. You have to put your mask on first before helping someone else. As an educator, if you are not taking care of yourself, how can you possibly help your students and colleagues?

I would ask that you commit to spending a few minutes each day on yourself. Schedule this in your calendar as a recurrent event and make sure to show up for this "appointment" each and every day.

SHOCKERS
Wrap-Up

---◆---

I guess I could have added an exclamation point at the end of SHOCKERS. This could have been for dramatic effect or to show how important each of these items is for helping all students to succeed.

With time, I'm sure that the SHOCKERS approach will grow and change. Perhaps the cute acronym, will become a very different word or even a phrase. My goal is to continue to fine tune this tool to make it as applicable and easy to implement as possible.

Behavior Overview

———————◆———————

Astudent with extreme behaviors can negatively impact a classroom environment and in some cases, an entire school. These disruptions can present safety challenges and prevent the student (and other students) from accessing the curriculum. There are a variety of causes of these behaviors, many of which are mental health, trauma, and/or environmentally related. Regardless of the cause of the behaviors, these situations require careful planning, compassion, and skill. A positive in dealing with children with explosive, challenging, and oppositional behaviors is that there are many strategies, tools, and interventions that have been implemented successfully to help reduce the behaviors and help improve the present and future outlook for the student.

Take a minute to think about a challenging student that you are working with now or one that you have worked with in the past. I want you to think about this student on his/her best day, working on his/her most preferred activity, and engaged in something that is tied to a relative strength. Write down all of the adjectives and descriptors that you can about this student as you are picturing him/her engaging in this activity. Now, I want you to think about the same student on his/her worst day, working on his/her least preferred activity, and engaged in something that is tied to an area of weakness. Now add adjectives and descriptors about this student as you picture him/her engaging in this activity.

What do you notice about your list? If yours is anything like my list, you will see positives and also negatives. How is this possible? How does this information help us determine the best strategies and interventions to support a student like this?

I use a similar activity when I do school and district trainings on trauma and challenging behaviors. The strange thing is that in a large room, you end up getting almost as many positive words as negative words. Additionally, you get words that can be both positive and negative based on the context and the situation. An example would be persistent. If you have a student who is refusing work or is non-compliant, the word persistent is not a positive. If you have the same student who is working on a complex math problem, the word persistent is a positive.

The reason for this activity is to realize that even the most challenging student has some positives, and positives equal potential and opportunity. This is also a great place to start when thinking about how to proceed with a challenging student. We want to identify their strengths, focus energy towards these strengths, and try to get a quick win. This process works especially well when the root cause of the behaviors has to do with poor self-image, fear of failure, lack of trust, or hopelessness.

Students that
Struggle with Behaviors

---◆---

Students that Struggle with Behaviors, Do So in One or More of the Following Ways:

1) Engine Always Running High and Short Fuse

The student arrives at school already at a level seven or eight on a scale of ten. This would be considered the student's norm or relative calm. The challenge with this is that any minor setback, annoyance, frustration, disappointment or change can set this student off and in a big way. The student's reaction would be thought of as an extreme overreaction to a minor item. In reality, there just is not as much wiggle room or a buffer.

2) Limited Coping Skills and Tools

The student has limited coping skills and few tools to use when frustrated, upset, annoyed or disappointed. As a result of having limited coping skills and few tools, the child reacts in a negative way. This may involve physical contact with staff or students, destruction of school work or other objects, use of inappropriate language, refusal to follow directions, and eloping from the classroom, area and/or school. This is similar to the idea that you use the tools that you have. If you need a screwdriver and only have a hammer, you will use the hammer. This may be ineffective and overkill, but what else can you do?

3) Lack of Ability to Self-Regulate

The student has limited or no ability to self-regulate emotions and/or calm down when they are frustrated, upset, annoyed, disappointed, or make a mistake. This situation may involve crying, shutting down, physical contact with staff or students, destruction of school work or other objects, use of inappropriate language, refusal to follow directions, and eloping from the classroom, area and/or school.

4) Negative Thinking and Lack of Hope

The student has negative thoughts and is lacking hope. This may be as a result of a difficult home life, trauma, or past disappointments. These negative thoughts interfere with the student's ability to complete school work, establish healthy relationships or take positive educational risks.

5) Fixed Mindset and Inflexible

The student has limited ability to "go with the flow" or accept change in an appropriate way. When faced with an unexpected change, this student reacts by shutting down. The student becomes unable to problem solve or discuss what they are feeling.

6) Poor Peer Relations and Difficulty Making Friends

The student may have exhibited inappropriate behaviors that make other students scared or reluctant to interact with them. In addition, the student may have poor social skills that further prevent existing peers and new peers from wanting to become friends with them. The lack of friends makes the student's situation more difficult. Adding to the student's challenges is a feeling of isolation and potentially a negative outlook.

7) Difficulty with Introspection and Empathy

The student has limited ability to reflect and articulate feelings, emotions, and/or actions. This relates to those internally and those in others. When this student makes a poor choice that impacts another student, it is very difficult for them to truly feel what the other student is feeling or to feel remorseful.

8) Lack of Social Skills

The student may have difficulty with social skills. This makes engaging in conversations, working appropriately with adults, and being accepted by others difficult. The lack of social skills also has the potential of escalating situations, due to the student's inability to accept "no" for an answer, disagree appropriately, or appropriately respond to an adult.

Effective Strategies

---•◆•---

So, What Does Work for Behaviors?

A) Stay Calm

Struggling students feed off of the actions, body language, and volume of others in their environment. This can either help reduce the issue or increase the intensity. A good first step is to at least outwardly appear to be calm, even if you are freaking out inside.

B) Work as a Team to Problem Solve and Create a Safety Plan

This is included in the "SHOCKERS" approach. Many minds are better than one. A team can help come up with a more robust list of possible interventions and strategies. The team can also come up with a plan that ensures the safety of the student, other students, and the staff members.

C) Be Proactive

We truly do not have a minute to waste. We also know that behaviors rarely solve themselves. Planning in advance is the best course of action. It is better to have over-planned than to be unprepared for a situation.

D) Document and Keep Good Data (Before, During and After)

We learn so much from our successes and also our failures. It is very important to document situations and behaviors before, during, and after a challenging situation. We can analyze these situations to better plan and predict future situations.

E) Do Not Take Things Personally (It is Not About You)

Nobody likes to be ignored, disrespected, or verbally attacked. As difficult as this is, we need to remember that this is not about you and not to take the situation personally. Students who are struggling will say and do unkind things. This is due to whatever they are struggling with internally or due to other environmental issues.

F) Focus on and Reinforce the Positives

It is easy to get sucked into focusing on the negatives. While it is important to be aware of negatives (or challenges) with a student, we have to remember that this is a child or teen and ensure that we focus on the positives. These positives provide an opportunity to build on for future situations.

G) Create a Safe and Quiet Space in the Room and Also a Buddy Classroom

I always told my staff that none of us receive "combat pay." I never want any of my staff or students to get hurt. In dealing with a struggling student, we need to have an escape and a choice that ensures safety for everyone. This may be a place in your room or a buddy classroom. In addition to identifying the safe and quiet place, it is essential to practice using these spaces when the student is calm.

H) Teach Social Skills

There are several models for teaching social skills. I believe that this needs to be a focused and deliberate instruction area for our students. Many of our students have not been taught social skill-related items that we take for granted. How can we expect the students to utilize these, if they have never been taught? Often time, a lack of a social skill is the starting point of a conflict with adults and peers. We can avoid this altogether, by teaching these social skills at an early age and reinforcing them regularly.

I) Identify the Captain of the Team (Critical Friend) to Build Relationships, Daily Check-in/out

As mentioned in the "SHOCKERS Approach," each student in a building needs to have a "critical friend." This one-minute daily check-in can really help a student with struggling behaviors; it can change their life-trajectory; and in some cases, may actually save a life!

J) Use Fewer Words

There are hundreds of thousands of words in the English language. When dealing with a struggling student, you don't need to use all of them. In reality, it is better to be concise and direct. This will eliminate the possibility of confusion. Struggling students will respond better when the instruction or choice is clear.

K) Include Stakeholders and Students in Creation of a Plan

This is similar to the schoolwide team in the "SHOCKERS" approach. Additionally, other stakeholders need to be included in the planning. This may include a parent or other significant person in a child's life. One planning meeting that I attended, involved the student's Tae Kwon Do instructor. He added a great deal of insight and it really helped to ensure that the plan was implemented with fidelity at school, at practice, and in the home. We also need to include the student in the planning. If the student is bought in, the plan is much more likely succeed.

L) Incorporate Daily Movement and Mindfulness Activities

Some students come to school in no shape to learn. Some are too high, some are too low, some have sensory input needs, and others just need help readjusting after a rough morning at home or on the bus. An investment of as little as fifteen minutes a day has been proven to significantly increase the likelihood of success for students.

M) Practice Self-care

Teaching is a very stressful career. Dealing with struggling and challenging students can impact the teacher in a negative way. Adding to this is the potential for secondary trauma when working with a student that has been traumatized. It is important to incorporate self-care techniques during the school day and at home. Another effective approach is to have a "self-care buddy" to work with and to check-in on each other. Many of the strategies that can be used for self-care, can also be taught to your students. Some teachers have successfully incorporated yoga, mindfulness, and movement into their daily classroom routine. This is a win-win for everyone!

N) Out of the Box Thinking

This is another letter from the "SHOCKERS" approach. Struggling students may require some out of the box strategies to help them find success. When successful, share these ideas with colleagues and consider creating a list of out of the box interventions. Also, consider discussing and sharing these items with other schools and districts from around the country. Why re-create the wheel?

O) Keep Adding Tools to your Toolbox

It is important in education, like other fields, to continue learning and acquiring new tools. Students are likely to keep coming to school with greater and more varied needs. The more tools you acquire (and share) the higher the likelihood of success. It may be a good idea to discuss the tools that you have and those that you need with your colleagues. Someone in your building will be a great resource for a particular tool. I think of this like building a home. I may be great at painting and poor and hanging drywall. I can support those that are not as great at painting and someone can help me with hanging drywall.

P) Monitor Progress and Modify Plan as Needed

As I stated earlier in the book, a good plan may not work right away, and a bad plan may work once and never again. It is important to adjust and adapt as needed. Some of the most effective strategies are those that have been adjusted and customized to the specific student.

Q) Clear and Concise Rules and Expectations

As a teacher, I had one rule—RESPECT. This was respect for self, others, objects, our time, etc. This clear rule along with other procedures were spelled out, taught, posted, and revisited frequently. Some challenging situations arise out of confusion, lack of clarity, or lack of practice. These are easy ones to eliminate.

R) Plan for Regular and Frequent Breaks

Different studies have concluded that the average attention span falls in the several minute range. This is challenging when schools are set-up for students to sit and to remain focused for long periods of time. Some behaviors are due to a student's inability to focus or attend for long periods of time. This can be resolved by building in regular and frequent breaks for the whole class or the individual student. I believe that the investment of time in breaks is far better than the loss of time due to challenging behaviors.

S) Plan for Transitions and Changes in Schedules/Routines

Change is hard for everyone. Some students struggle with transitions and changes. These can be and should be planned for as much as possible. It can be as simple as keeping a visual schedule and letting students know of changes to the schedule/routine in advance.

T) Focus on Behavior Not the Student

I still believe that there are no bad students. There are students with behaviors that we do not like, but no bad students. If we believe this, we need to use language that focuses on the behavior that is unacceptable while still ensuring that the student knows that they are valued, cared about, and loved.

U) Listen and Look for Triggers

Often there are signs, signals, and triggers that can be avoided or eliminated from your classroom or school. These are a gift from the student. They are telling you that if this, then this. If we take away the antecedent or cause, we may very well eliminate the behaviors. This goes beyond words. Look at facial expression and body language. Some students fidget right before they "lose it". Know the "tell" and you can avoid the explosion.

V) Help Identify and Implement Replacement Behaviors

Anger, sadness, frustration, and lack of flexibility are very normal human behaviors and actions. The important part is how we deal with these emotions. Some struggling students choose to hit, kick, punch, bite, throw things, and elope from the classroom or school. We want to help train the student to deal with their emotions is a more safe and desirable way. One example is the student that elopes from the classroom (the flight response). We can train them to run to a safe place. Additionally, the student that acts out physically, can be trained to throw a soft ball against the wall or to squeeze a stress ball, instead of harming another student or staff person.

W) Build the Bank Account with Student and Family with Positive Interactions

A struggling student's family can become your best partner or your biggest challenge. It is so important to build the bank account with "positive deposits" right away before you have to make a "negative withdrawal" from the account. In so many cases, what you are seeing at school also has been a problem in the past and also at home. If we build the bank account, we can add stakeholders to our team that already know what works and what does not work.

X) Involve Therapy and Mental Health Resources

The education and mental health fields overlap a great deal. Many of us received very little training in these areas as an education student. Therapists and other mental health professionals are amazing resources for training or as an on-going resource. There are programs, such as Distinguished School of Mental Health and Wellness (DSMHW) that provides intensive training for school staff. Whether it is DSMHW or another resource, these are well worth the time investment to be best able to support all of your students.

Y) Build Hope for the Future

The letter "H" in "SHOCKERS Approach" is for hope. There is nothing more important than helping a student to have hope for the future. Even in a very small way, if you can help a student to have things to look forward to, you can change their life trajectory. You may also save a life!

Z) Give More Responsibility than What is Deserved

In an earlier chapter, we discussed Mikey. This was a great example of a student rising to our expectations and really stepping-up when given a greater responsibility than his prior behaviors warranted. You will be surprised what a student will do when given the opportunity to do so.

I ran out of letters above, so I am including a couple other thoughts/suggestions. I would recommend focusing on using behavior challenges as learning experiences, rather than as a punitive approach. I would also advocate for looking at a restorative approach as a building-wide focus. It seems logical to me that we look at ways to repair what has been done, to help both the victim and the aggressor, and find a win-win for re-entry into the classroom or school community.

Ineffective Strategies

———•◆•———

<u>What Doesn't Work for Behaviors?</u>

In the past section, I shared many strategies that are effective for students that struggle with behaviors. I also want to include strategies that are NOT effective for students that struggle with behaviors. Before I list these items, I believe it is important to stress that we should abandon these practices. Why would we continue to use strategies that are, at best, ineffective and, at worst, very harmful to students? I would recommend that you think about your intended goal for a strategy or consequence and then determine what the desired outcome is for this strategy or consequence. From there, look for evidence-based practices that best align with the desired goal and outcome.

Below are some examples of strategies that are not effective:

1) Yelling at Students

Yelling at a student is both disrespectful and ineffective. Many of our students are yelled at regularly at home. Students learn to tune this out and stop listening. If this is disrespectful and ineffective, there is no reason to continue this practice. There are many other ways to get your point across without yelling at a student.

2) Paddling a Student

I was completely shocked to find out that paddling (or corporal punishment) is still legal in the State of Missouri. I would imagine this is the case in other states as well. In Missouri, it is the local school district that determines if this is a practice that is allowed. There are public and private schools across the country that still allow this practice. There is zero evidence supporting this as an effective strategy for dealing with a struggling student. I think about a student that is misbehaving due to trauma or abuse. I question this practice and would advocate for abolishing it immediately.

3) Making a Student Lose Face in Front of Their Peers

If you want a guaranteed escalation of behavior, I would recommend you do something that causes a student to lose face in front of their peers. For many of our students, they have very little except their dignity and self-esteem. Making a student lose face in front of their peers is wrong, mean-spirited, and highly ineffective. I would recommend having conversations quietly and away from the student's peers.

4) Taking Away Movement Activities

A student that struggles with making the right choice, may also be the student that struggles with having too much energy or a mental health concern. For so many students with similar challenges, a great strategy is to break up the day with movement. As mentioned earlier in the book, it is very hard for everyone to sit and focus for prolonged periods. So, I question why we take away opportunities for students to move and to get this energy out.

5) Punishment or Consequence Given in Anger

I have always told my staff that if they are red in the face and their hands are clenched, this is the wrong time to be handing out a consequence. Additionally, when you are angry, this is a great time to get help from a colleague or administrator. If you give out a punishment or consequence when you are angry, it will almost always lead to an undesired outcome. This is similar to a parent telling their child that they are grounded for life. As soon as a statement like this is made, both you and the student know that this will never be enforced. It would definitely be appropriate and more desirable to tell the student that you will need to think about and then discuss the consequence later.

6) Threats of Punishments

This one goes along with giving consequences when angry. If you threaten something, you need to follow through on it. If you don't, this makes you lose credibility with the student and will also cause you greater challenges in the future. A much better approach is to clearly state items as if/then (i.e. If you choose to continue this behavior, then the consequence will be…).

7) Disproportionate Consequences

I was asked to do a training for school administrators in a northeastern city. The purpose of my visit was to help a few of the administrators move towards appropriate, fair, and logical consequences. Previously, these administrators gave out consequences to set an example for the other students. The rationale was that if they come down hard on a few students, it would discourage other students from doing the same behavior. In many cases, these were disproportionate and strictly punitive. There are many reasons why this was a problem. One item that stuck out to me was how these disproportionate consequences went almost exclusively to students in lower socio-economic groups. More affluent students with similar behaviors (i.e. vaping, cheating on a test, stealing) were given a slap on the wrist. This was unethical, unfair, and had the impact of negatively impacting a student's life trajectory. For many students, nationally, this is a practice that expedites the school to prison pipeline. This practice needs to end right away.

8) Suspensions

This is the most tricky and controversial one on the list. When I lead a training, anywhere in America, this is the item that gets the most support and also the most pushback. There is zero evidence anywhere that shows that suspensions work. They do not. This is even more the case when a student is dealing with a mental health or trauma related issue. Suspensions cause a great deal of harm. I can't think of a single student that returned from a suspension, better than when they left. The challenge is that in some cases students need to go home (i.e. a student punches another student and breaks their nose; a student brings a weapon to school; a student is intoxicated or high at school...). This item could be a discussion topic for a semester long graduate class. I will stand-by my statement that suspensions are ineffective and we need to use them only as a last option. Additionally, we need to work on suspension alternatives and also look for ways to be pro-active with students that struggle with behaviors.

I am sure there are many other examples of strategies that are not effective. If you can think of any, I would like to hear them from you. Perhaps they will be included in the next version of this book or another book.

Conclusion

———◆———

I shared many stories and scenarios in this book. I also shared tools, interventions, resources, and ideas. I hope you will leave this reading experience with an idea or two that can benefit you as an educator and students. If it helps one student, I will be very happy that writing this book (a labor of love) was well worth the effort.

Students are coming to our schools with so many challenges and concerns. Each of them is unique in their own way and the challenges of problem solving and helping students presents an amazing opportunity for a team to collaborate. I encourage your team to work together, have cognitive conflicts, problem solve, and keep caring. Our students need and deserve this.

The job as an educator can be very overwhelming and frustrating. But the fruit of your labor can be something that is truly amazing. You have the most important job in the world. Keep your chin up and keep fighting the good fight for our kids! We can do this—together!

I want to encourage you to stand for what you believe in and fight tooth and nail for what is best for your students. Figure out what your non-negotiables are and stick to your guns. Let everyone know that fair is not always equal. Ensure that we give students what they need, when they need it. Most of all remember that there are no bad kids!

I hope to see you in the trenches in the upcoming months or years. I plan to continue my training tour across the country. It is my goal to positively impact 100,000 educators and a million students. If I can be of any assistance, please do not hesitate to reach out!

Overlap of Education and Mental Health

---◆---

"Students that act out are doing us a favor. They're telling us that something is wrong. I worry about the quiet and compliant student that is secretly hurting inside and wondering if it is worth living... And we have no idea!" **-Dr. Bryan Pearlman**

M y wife Lena and I have worked in our respective fields for the past twenty-five years. For the majority of this time, we each worked in our own silo with very little overlap. We each had our own work world, our own acronyms, our own challenges, and even our own tools.

Lena's silo as a mental health therapist involved providing therapy and counseling services to children and teens who were struggling with stress, anxiety, depression, anger, and relationship challenges. Her goal was to help each of these individuals live life to the fullest, to be happy, and to be mentally healthy. Her tools included: cognitive behavior therapy (CBT), dialectical behavior therapy (DBT), Gestalt therapy, motivational interviewing, and mindfulness. Lena's services were provided in hospitals, community organizations, and then finally in her own private practice.

As a teacher, my world revolved around helping students to grow and learn each day. I was responsible for twenty-five fifth-grade students at a time. Later as an administrator, my "classroom" became significantly larger and I worked hard to ensure that both students and adults achieved to their highest potential (and that everyone played nice together). A significant portion of my time was spent managing behaviors and processing students. I told colleagues that I often felt like either a busy New York City Deli or a hospital triage department. There was never a shortage of customers and always a line. The tools that I had at my disposal were mostly carrots and sticks. I tried to change behaviors with an incentive to comply (carrot) or the fear of a consequence (stick). I had many repeat customers and several that made little or no improvement in their behaviors. My carrots and sticks really were not that effective for these students.

As time passed, our silos began creeping closer together. The therapy silo and the educator silo started to overlap. The silos began to look more like a Venn diagram. Our conversations started to have common language from our respective fields. We both spoke about students who were struggling with trauma, those with self-harming behaviors, those that were missing school because of anxiety or depression, and those with suicidal ideation or attempts.

The two of us spent a great deal of time thinking about how we could utilize our combined experiences, skills, and training to help these students that were struggling in school and in life. We decided that the overlapping portion of the Venn diagram is where our focus had to be. We also agreed that we had to do something and soon. We could not waste a minute. Time is too precious, and we could improve the quality of life for so many children, teens, and their families (and potentially save many lives as well).

Lena and I spent the next year researching the overlapping areas. Through this research, we found data and statistics that painted an even more bleak picture. The suicide rate for students was at an all-time high, a growing percentage of students with mental health concerns were receiving little or no treatment, and there was a significant number of traumatized students that were being suspended from school due to behaviors. This information further cemented and reinforced our need to act.

Our conversations led to meetings with friends and colleagues. We sought out those from related fields: psychiatrists, pediatricians, educators, therapists, counselors, and professors. The discussions focused on disrupting the status-quo with a solution-focused approach. These friends and colleagues shared many great ideas, and each articulated the desire to be involved in this effort.

The product of these discussions led to the establishment of the national non-profit organization "**Distinguished School of Mental Health and Wellness**" (DSMHW). We decided that our impact would be greatest if we could work with school staff, administration, families, and the community to ensure that they all had the tools necessary to meet the growing mental health needs of their students. It was critically important that all stakeholders were involved and committed to this important mission. We developed a national standard of what a "distinguished school" would look like and created evidence-based training modules to cover the critical areas of mental health that most impact students, staff, schools, and the community (trauma, stress/anxiety, oppositional/challenging behaviors, depression, self-harm/suicide, mindfulness, educator self-care). The twelve-month training process that we developed involves data collection, conducting a specific needs assessment for the school, several on-site visits, video trainings/conversations, and the development of SMART goals. At the end of the twelve-month process, schools that achieve their goals will be nationally certified and recognized as a Distinguished School of Mental Health & Wellness. More information about DSMHW is available at: DSMHW.org

Acknowledgements

I want to thank my wife Lena. She has been incredibly supportive of all my efforts over the years (the good ideas and even the not so good ideas). I would not be where I am without her love and support! Her knowledge and experience in mental health has led to many of the strategies and ideas that I have incorporated into my work with struggling students. It is a blessing that I get to live and work together with my wife (and best friend).

I want to thank my children, Samantha and Matthew, for being the greatest gifts that I have ever received. They are great examples of kind, caring, compassionate, and hard-working people. They have such amazing futures and I look forward to seeing how they do their part to change the world for the better!

I want to thank my parents for all of the sacrifices they made along the way to help me and my siblings to find success. All of their children are successful educators with advanced degrees.

Professionally, there are way too many people for me to thank. I have had the honor to work with so many talented educators. Thank you to all who have been a part of this amazing journey!

To all of my students, you have left a permanent imprint in my mind, heart, and soul. I wish only the best for each and every one of you. I will always be here for you.

References

Ablon, J. S. (2018). *Changeable: The surprising science behind helping anyone change.* New York: TarcherPerigee.

Burke Harris, N., MD. (2014). How childhood trauma affects health across a lifetime. [Video File]. Retrieved from: https://www.ted.com/talks/nadine_burke_harris_how_childhood_trauma_affects_health_across_a_lifetime/up-next?language=en

Greene, R. (2008). *Lost at School: Why our kids with behavioral challenges are falling through the cracks.* New York: Scribner.

Petrow, S. (2018, October 27). How a 'Kindness Contagion' Improves Lives, Especially Now. *The Washington Post.*

Robinson, K. (2006, February). Do schools kill creativity? [Video file]. Retrieved from:
https://www.ted.com/talks/ken_robinson_says_schools_kill_creativity?language=en

About the Author

———————◆———————

D r. Bryan Pearlman is a veteran educator, administrator, and keynote speaker. He is the founder of Most Valuable Professional Development, LLC (MostValuablePD.com) and the co-founder of the non-profit Distinguished School of Mental Health and Wellness (DSMHW.org). His expertise is ensuring all children succeed, challenging behaviors, trauma, and differentiation. Dr. Pearlman is on a mission to help 100,000 educators and a million students.

Contact

Dr. Bryan Pearlman can be reached at:

Email:
bryan@MostValuablePD.com

Phone:
314-455-4347

Twitter:
@DrP_Principal